Children
in the
Shadows

Children in the Shadows

Ruth Jaeger Buntain

Review and Herald Publishing Association
Washington, D.C. 20012

Editor: Bobbie Jane Van Dolson
Book Design: Rudolf Varesko
Cover Design: Robert Wright
Cover Illustration: Mary Cabrera

Type Set: 11/12 Souvenir Light

Printed in U.S.A.

Bible text credited to N.E.B. is from *The New English Bible.*
Copyright © The Delegates of the Oxford University Press
and the Syndics of the Cambridge University Press 1961,
1970. Reprinted by permission.

Library of Congress Cataloging in Publication Data

Buntain, Ruth Jaeger.
    Children in the shadows.

    1. Parent and child. 2. Child psychology.
3. Loneliness in children. I. Title.
HQ755.85.B86   1982   649'.1   82-13230
ISBN 0-8280-0146-4

Contents

Parental Shadows

*I*n a much-loved poem for children, Robert Louis Stevenson wrote, "I have a little shadow that goes in and out with me." To have been more accurate, he should have written, "I have three little shadows," for every child is followed closely by his own shadow and the invisible ones of his parents.

Wherever the child goes, these parental shadows accompany him. Even at the schoolhouse they do not remain outside the door, but follow the child into the classroom, down the aisle, to his desk. They are unseen enrollees, and wise teachers are aware of their presence, never underestimating their influence.

During my many years of teaching, the shadows of several thousands of parents affected my classrooms. Some of these encouraged scholastic achievement and balanced personality development. Others were ominous, inviting child failure and maladjustment.

As a result of my contacts with these parental shadows, one fact above all others has impressed me. Never do parents influence a child as potently as they do during the formative years. As Ellen White states: "The lessons learned, the habits formed, during the years of infancy and childhood, have more to do with the formation of the character and the direction of the life than have all the instruction and training of after years."—*The Ministry of Healing,* p. 380.

I remember the forces that were shaping Floyd, a pupil in one of my second-grade classes. I could not ignore the shadow that followed him to school, the influence of a mother who was beautiful, socially ambitious, and resentful of her children. She belonged to the feed-them-and-leave-them school of thought, those parents who think they have done their duty when they have provided for children's physical needs, but who are unaware of or indifferent to the hunger that cannot be appeased with bread.

Floyd was a handsome, intelligent, disturbed child. He should have been an advanced student, but because of emotional problems, he was trailing the class. He had frequent temper tantrums and sometimes gasped for breath. "Something's wrong with my breathing," he would tell me. Something *was* wrong. But it wasn't in the lungs. A medical examination proved that.

After I had told the class a story Floyd often made such comments as "If I had been there I would have killed him" or "I would have taken out a knife and cut off his head."

Floyd frequently came to school without breakfast. "Mother didn't get up," he would explain as he walked into the classroom, munching a cookie. Her name often appeared in the society columns. She headed many drives. But she was never home when the children came from school. The woman who took care of the house was there, but she was busy with the mops and brooms.

Floyd's mother was married to her fourth husband, Floyd's stepfather. The boy was always worried about his own father. He couldn't remember having seen him. He would come to me and say, "The father I'm living with isn't my own father. He's just my stepfather. I don't know where my dad is. Bob's father comes to see him, but I never see my dad."

Sometimes when Floyd became too disturbed I'd say, "Why don't you go to the easel and paint a picture?" While he painted, the gaspy breathing would subside. As he splashed his inner turmoil onto the paper he would become calmer. But the pictures weren't calm. They were stormy drawings featuring heavy, tangled lines, like piles of barbed wire.

Every child needs to feel that his parents want, enjoy, and love him, and Floyd knew that nobody at home really cared. And what he knew, thousands of other children also know. Home is too often the place where parents change clothes before running away from their children, away from themselves. Shadows from such homes darken classrooms. They can blur the words in the readers. They can make unintelligible the numbers in the arithmetic books.

There has been a too-prevalent belief in Western countries—and in some professedly Christian households—that a good home is to be judged by how many cars there are in the garage and how many of the latest appliances are in the kitchen. In reality, a good home is where spiritual and moral values are emphasized and where no substitutes are offered for love.

Closely related to the feed-them-and-leave-them parents are the too-busy parents. These may be sincerely interested in their families, but they permit too many encroachments to come between them and those who are closest to them. They are so busy that they have little time for their children. The shadows cast by such parents accompanied Mabel to school and adversely affected her scholastic achievement.

At the beginning of the term when Mabel was in my class, each child made a folder in which he was to save his work, samples of what he had been doing, to show the parents what had been accomplished at school.

The time came to take the folders home. When they were distributed the children clapped as youngsters do when they are happy or excited. The folders were treasures to them, and they were shiny-eyed as they started homeward. Obviously they believed their papers would be treasures to their parents, as they should have been.

No child left the classroom with more stars in her eyes than did Mabel. No one hurried home faster than she.

The next morning I asked, "How did your parents like your folder, Mabel?"

"They didn't even look at it. They said they were too busy."

How little time it would have taken to inspect the papers and compliment Mabel on her workmanship. How encouraging it would have been to her if Mother had hung some of the papers on the wall or perhaps started a scrapbook in which to keep samples, and to which they could have added in the future. But these parents were too busy to give consideration to their daughter's accomplishments.

Perhaps next time Mabel won't bother to take home a folder. Somewhere between the school and the house, she will discard the results of her efforts. If nobody at homes cares, why should she? There will be no more stars in her eyes.

In the future some of these too-busy parents will find that they have time—time to appear at juvenile court or to sit in a counselor's office to discuss an emotionally disturbed child.

The time to establish parental rapport with children is during the early years of childhood. These are the years when habits, attitudes, and character are being determined. In later years, the too-busy people may find that they have time, but they will also discover that it will be too late.

There are other unfortunate parental shadows. The teacher sees Ned sitting in the last seat of the last row, and she sees more than Ned. She sees a father with pugilistic inclinations who is always telling his son, "Hold your own. Stand up and fight. If you don't knock him down I'll knock you down for not knocking him down." And she knows why Ned is in so many fights.

She sees Sadie sitting in the middle of some other row, but she sees more than Sadie. She remembers what the child said to her one afternoon while getting special help after school.

"I have three daddies. One went away and two are in jail. Now Joe is with us."

"Is Joe your new daddy?"

"I don't know if Mamma married him or not. My first daddy took a car that didn't belong to him and is in jail. My second daddy got drunk all the time and is in jail. Once when he got drunk he threw coffee all over the house, and my grandma had to call the cops. My third daddy went away. Mamma got mad and made him leave. Now Joe is at our house."

The teacher sees Tim writing numbers at the board, but she also sees the shadow of his mother beside him. No matter how many numbers Tim writes correctly, the score will not please his mother. No matter how hard he works, the results will be unsatisfactory. For the woman in the shadows is a reflection of the we-want-perfection parents, parents who are overly concerned about their own competitive standing. Because of this, they often encourage their children to compete with one another, as well as with the children next door. We-want-perfection parents are determined that their children succeed where they themselves have failed. They project on youth their own unfilled expectations.

Not a school term has passed but some child has said to me, "If I get all A's, I'll get a present."

"If I pass, I'll get a bicycle."

"I'm going to get a dollar for every good mark on my card."

In offering their children money for good grades, parents show a lack of understanding. Although children should be encouraged to do their best, and less than their best should not be acceptable, parents should realize that scholastic achievement is not something to be purchased like a pair of shoes or a dress. It is cruel and disheartening to a child to offer him gifts for a type of success that his limitations, and not his lack of application, make impossible for him to attain.

It would take volumes to record the unhappy effects on children of their exposure to cultural patterns that put more emphasis on getting ahead than on acquiring character and spiritual values. Such an emphasis means that the laggers and the less-attractive youngsters who fall behind and are unable to compensate in acceptable ways for their inadequacies are the children who are neglected and bypassed by their parents and too often by their teachers.

Children should be judged and guided on an individual basis, with the recognition that each child is a separate entity possessing a unique set of potentialities. There can be no mass production in the field of child development. Each child has his special aptitudes and special limitations that must be kept in mind in making a total appraisal.

More Shadows

*T*here are other unfortunate parental shadows that follow children into the classroom. A particularly oppressive type is that projected by smother-parents. These attempt to do their children's thinking, make their decisions, and choose their careers.

Freddy was the child of a smother-mother. He was a likeable boy with latent talents, a charming smile, gentle ways, and a subdued spirit.

Freddy's mother knew how and what I should teach. She knew in which readers Freddy should be reading. She knew what grades he should have. When tests were given and Freddy mentioned them at home she was often at school the next day to see his paper, making sure that nothing had been marked wrong that should have been marked right. I was young and inexperienced and too apprehensive to let her know that her attitudes and actions were out of place.

Freddy's mother haunted me, and she must have haunted him. He did not use the fine mind that God had given him. He never had an opportunity to use it. His thinking and his life were as carefully laid out as a road map lays out highways and towns.

Freddy's mother came to school too often. She interrupted my lessons. She would sit there watching me teach and then call out a suggestion or offer some advice.

Once she visited during a discussion of the San Francisco Bay Bridge. In the middle of class she called out, "We recently went over that bridge. This would be a good time to have Freddy tell about his experience."

Obediently I asked, "Freddy, would you like to tell us about your ride over the bridge?"

And just as obediently he answered, "Yes, ma'am," and trotted to the front of the room.

Fortunately, few smother-mothers go to the extremes that Freddy's mother did. This is fortunate for the child, the school, and for everyone else who comes within the radius of their blighting personalities.

A pamphlet on child guidance published by the National Association for Mental Health says, "Every child needs to know that his parents want him to grow up and that they encourage him to try new things . . . that they have confidence in his ability to do things for himself and by himself."

It is a terrible thing to dominate a child's thinking, to make all his decisions, to stunt his ability to reach successful conclusions. The results reach even more tragic proportions when that child becomes an adult incapable of solving his own problems. When decisions must be reached he tries to imagine what his mother would say or do—or his father or whoever dominated his thinking. Such a person is often doomed to a life of vacillation, putting off (until a tomorrow that never comes) the decisions that should be made today.

From an early age children should be guided to make choices, to reach conclusions. Even the very young child can have a voice in matters that affect him. Obviously, the decision making should be appropriate to his age and comprehension.

For instance, a child does not have a choice between whether or not to play in the street, or whether or not to go to the dentist, or whether to eat junk food or that which is more nutritious. But even a 3-year-old can be given a choice between a red toothbrush and a green one. And he can decide which of his favorite stories he would like to have read at bedtime.

A 5-year-old can choose the kind of seed to plant in his garden. Would he like a dog for a pet, or would he prefer a cat?

A 10-year-old boy can rightfully be assigned to mow the lawn and weed the garden. But he might be given the choice as to when to do it. Will it be in the morning or the afternoon? On Monday or Tuesday?

When children have made their choices, they should be held accountable for the consequences insofar as is reasonable. If Mary chose the dress with ruffles instead of the one with pleats, she should be required to wear it even though she later regrets her choice. If Tom decided to mow the lawn on Tuesday instead of Monday, he should be held to his decision even though a friend phones and invites him to go on a hike. At least he should finish his work before he goes on the outing.

Wise parents give their children as many opportunities as possible to make choices and to reach decisions. This develops a sense of responsibility and increases self-confidence. It lays a foundation for future years when more consequential choices will have to be made. Then the issue will not be what color toothbrush to select, but, rather, whether to marry Tom or John. Whether to go to a trade school or to college. Whether to continue living in Vernal or to move to Phoenix. The children of smother-parents, those whose ability to reach conclusions was undermined, will not have it easy when they confront the choices of adulthood.

There is another parental type that casts an unfortunate shadow on a child. This is the shadow reflected by the you're-not-going-to-get-hurt variety of parents. Often these are parents who knew poverty and abuse when they were children. The deprivation and mistreatment they experienced left wounds that will never heal. Plastic surgeons can remove surface scars, but there are no surgeons, however skillful, who can completely remove the emotional scars of childhood.

These parents do everything within their power to see that their children experience nothing of unhappiness and that they get everything they want. Timmy Brown's father was one of these parents. As a child Mr. Brown had known poverty and neglect. When his friends went on outings, he had to stay home and work in the fields. When they received parental love, he received abuse. As an adult Mr. Brown resolved that his children would never want for anything.

Consequently the Brown youngsters had more clothes, more playthings, and more spending money than they needed. When the weather was warm Timmy's father often came to school at noon with an ice-cream bar or a cold drink for his son. When

Timmy joined the school band, Daddy bought him one of the most expensive horns obtainable.

This didn't go over too well with the other children. Who did Timmy think he was, getting all that special attention and all those fancy things? His peers resented him more than they liked him. They didn't know about the scars in his father's heart. And the father didn't know that in giving his children too much he was sowing the seeds for the very kind of unhappiness he wanted to prevent.

You're-not-going-to-get-hurt parents go to extremes to shield their children from rebuffs and hurts that come to everyone in the course of daily living. They do not prepare their children for the inevitable day when the apron strings will be cut, when the parents will no longer be there to insulate against realities. And no one else will be there either, to protect them against environmental thorns.

Children are not conditioned for good mental health by having their problems removed. They are rightly conditioned when they are guided to face and solve problems. They must be prepared for life as it is, not the way they might wish it were. They must be conditioned to disappointments as well as to victories, to humiliation as well as to exhilaration.

In discussing the mounting toll of emotional illness in the United States, Dr. Roy W. Menninger, president of the Menninger Foundation and member of the President's Commission on Mental Health, estimates that between 10 and 15 percent of the population have serious mental illness and that 70 percent of the population are adversely affected from time to time by the problems of living. In all probability many persons who are emotionally ill were not conditioned in childhood to meet life's disappointments with courage and optimism.

"Beyond the discipline of the home and the school, all have to meet the stern discipline of life. How to meet this wisely is a lesson that should be made plain to every child and to every youth. It is true that God loves us, that He is working for our happiness, and that, if His law had always been obeyed, we should never have known suffering; and it is no less true that, in this world, as the result of sin, suffering, trouble, burdens, come to every life. We may do the children and the youth a lifelong good by teaching them to meet bravely these troubles and burdens. While we should give them sympathy, let it never be such as to foster self-pity. What they need is that which stimulates and strengthens rather than weakens."—*Child Guidance,* p. 157.

Obviously, conditioning a child to meet "the stern discipline of life" should be done at the level of his stage of development, commensurate with his age and understanding. A very young child can be conditioned to accept the loss of loved ones—one of the harshest disciplines of life—by the wise way his parents handle his grief at the loss of a pet. The death of a pet can also be the means of orienting the religious implications of death.

Many parents condition their children to deny death as adults. They shield the young from its reality. They deny their children the experience that would orient them toward the acceptance of bereavement.

When services were held for Ken Lawson, a person known to the author, his 9-year-old daughter was not present.

On the morning of the funeral Ken's widow telephoned a friend. "Marge," she said, "may I ask a favor of you? I'd rather Nell didn't attend the funeral. She's too young. Will you please take her and plan something special?"

Marge took Nell. And while other family members were sharing an experience of closeness and caring, Nell was at the zoo. While the minister spoke words of comfort and hope, she was looking at the zebras, the lions, and the elephants.

Was Nell being prepared for the acceptance of bereavement in later years? If she should lose a husband or a child, would she be oriented to the implications of death and its acceptance? Or would she be conditioned to the denial of reality?

Joshua Liebman, in his book *Peace of Mind,* refers to the unwise way in which many adults handle the grief situation for their children:

"There is more human misery prevalent in the world because of the fallacious approach that adults take to children on the death problem than we would ever imagine. This is what frequently happens. A father dies, leaving a young child and a widow. At the time of the funeral the little boy is sent to some strange relative and the widowed mother and all the relatives conspire to conceal from

16

the child the true situation. The father's name is not mentioned or, if mentioned, the conversation is quickly turned to some other channel. The theory behind all this conspiracy of silence about the death of the father is that the little boy should be shielded from grief and pain. 'He is too young to know the truth.' This whole process of concealment, while motivated by the highest intentions, can prove to be terribly distorting to the child's emotional development."

"Now, I do not mean to imply that children have to be told the details about death . . . . The story of life and death must be told on their level of comprehension and in their child's frame of reference. . . . A child's mind should never be needlessly frightened. All this is true, but what is a supreme illusion among men is the idea that children cannot stand grief and sadness, that under all circumstances they must be coddled and sheltered against the winds of reality. No, the truth lies in exactly the opposite direction. The child can stand tears but not treachery, sorrow but not deceit. The little boy or girl should be dealt with in a straightforward, honest fashion; he should be allowed to share and participate in the family's woes as well as triumphs." *

If children are permitted this kind of participation, they will be oriented to the acceptance of misfortune in later years.

---

*Pages 126, 127, 130, 131. Copyright 1946 by Joshua Loth Liebman, renewed 1973 © by Fran Liebman. Reprinted by permission of Simon and Schuster, a division of Gulf & Western Corporation.

Lonely Children

One day while the pupils in my second-grade class were singing a folk song, Diana got out of her seat and came to me.

"Don't sing this song," she said gravely. "It makes me remember when we were all together. We used to sing it when we lived in the mountains. Before Mommy left us."

Diana was one of the Nation's many lonely children. She was lonely for the parent who had deserted her.

Loneliness is a plague that afflicts the entire human race. It is no respecter of persons or of age. Medical authorities agree that it affects even those in the cradle. Deprivation dwarfism, the medical term for lack of love, has been responsible for the death of many infants.

According to Lytt I. Gardner, a pediatrician at the Upstate Medical Center at the State University of New York, lack of love is a disease that used to kill most of the children in orphanages. The doctor reported that as late as 1915, 90 percent of the children in Baltimore orphanages died within the first year of admission from lack of love.

Dr. Gardner presented the case history of a mother who had given birth to twins, a boy and a girl. The boy was growing normally and was a little ahead of his sister.

Four months later the mother found that she was pregnant again. About this time her husband lost his job and deserted his family.

The woman transferred the hostility she felt toward her husband to her son. She withdrew her attention from him and withheld her affection. The child became a typical "thin dwarf." When he was a little more than a year old his height was that of a 7-month-old infant.

Unfortunately, as Dr. Gardner pointed out, when affection and love have been withheld from a child for any length of time, he never completely catches up mentally or physically, for companionship, devotion, and belonging are basic human needs.

"In the accounts of their childhood that neurotic clients give me," wrote the Swiss psychiatrist Paul Tournier in his book *Escape From Loneliness,* "the most constant theme is that of not having been loved by their parents. If we could question these parents, doubtless the father and mother would protest by enumerating all the sacrifices they made for their children.

" 'We were always given money when what we wanted was love,' a young woman told me. Another, a young man who had failed to turn up for an exam, ran to his father's office. He was made to wait, just like a client, and warned by his father that he was very pressed for time, even when he did get in to see him. Thus the son doubts his father's love, while the father is actually hiding his emotions under the cloak of business." [1]

One can sense the loneliness of the many children in America who are the victims of divorce. "Sorrow comes to all men," Abraham Lincoln once said, "and to the young it comes with bitterest agony, because it takes them unawares."

"Whom do you want to live with?" the child may be asked when he is told his parents are separating. "With Mother or Daddy?"

When the child chooses Mother, he is lonely for Daddy. When he chooses Daddy, he is lonely for Mother.

In Greenbrae, California, a five-year study was made on the children of divorced parents. The children studied were 3 to 18 years old at the time of divorce. They were from predominantly white middle-class families. With few exceptions the youngsters reacted to their parents' separation with anxiety and stress. Their recurring worries were about who would take care of them and whether their relationship with their parents would last.

Teachers who were questioned about the children's reactions to the divorces noted sadness or depression in many of the children. More than half of them showed unaccustomed restlessness.[2]

And even where there has been no divorce or separation, many children are lonely because both parents are working. There are 30 million children of working mothers in this Nation. The majority of these are key-chain children, those who go to school with a chain about their neck, to which is attached a key to the house.

When these children come home after school, no one is there to greet them. Often they would like to share with their mother something that happened at school—but she is not there. Often they would like to unburden to her a heart anxiety, a matter that might seem trivial to an adult but to them is a matter of great importance—but she is not there. These children are unattended and unsupervised. If they want to hear a human voice or have human companionship, they turn the dial of the television.

Because the largest increase in working mothers is among those with children under 6, enrollment of this age group in child-care centers is escalating. The roots of considerable school failure, misbehavior, and ill health are laid when children barely beyond the toddler stage are removed from the attachments of home and placed with groups of their age-mates.

There are sound reasons for placing some preschoolers in child-care centers or with other caretakers. This is particularly true when parents are mentally, morally, or emotionally unfit. But under normal circumstances home is the best place for young children. Preschool-care agencies cannot provide the warmth and attachment and personal attention that children need. It should also be kept in mind that often the character standards of those who care for the children differ from the home standards.

Tension may be created, with resultant stress for the child, when caretakers have ways of managing and disciplining that are different from those of the parents. While the child is away from home he is subjected to one kind of management. When he returns home he is subjected to another. The two may be in conflict. These are not easy adjustments for young children to make, and may predispose the child to nervous and emotional ills.

The parade of lonely children marches on. There is Matt, who has a harelip. He is often teased by his brothers, sisters, and classmates.

Jason is failing to achieve the goals set for him by his parents and is compared unfavorably with his siblings. They have been endowed by heredity with the potential for academic success. He hasn't, but no matter. He is made to feel that he is a disappointment to his family.

There is Michelle, who is terrified nightly by fighting parents. She lies on her cot in the darkness, trembling at the harsh words she hears her father and mother shouting at each other.

There is Jane, who returned to school after a three-week absence. "The reason I was gone so long is we moved away so my mother could get away from my daddy. But he came to Oakland too, and started hitting my mother. She had to call the cops. Now we're living with my grandmother. When we live with her my daddy doesn't hit my mother."

Some children live in homes where there is a great distance between the parents and the children, where there are barriers of coldness and reserve. These parents make no effort to really know their children, to understand their dispositions and draw out what is in their heart. They do nothing to answer their children's need for companionship or their yearning for sympathy and closeness.

Dr. Norman Vincent Peale, writing on runaways in an article in *Guideposts* magazine (July, 1978), stated that he has always felt that the basic reason a child leaves home is unhappiness that corrodes into anger. This is a deep anger resulting from absence of love, understanding, communication, and sometimes, strangely, the absence of discipline.

Youth are searching for these things when they leave home, Dr. Peale feels. When one young runaway was picked up by the police, she said that she was actually looking for a home. She was from an upper-middle-class family, as are many runaways. This girl, feeling that she had lost contact with her parents and could not make herself understood, was compelled to turn her back on them and their way of life.

As a result of his contacts with many runaways, Dr. Peale offers some suggestions to parents. Although they are specifically offered to parents of teen-agers, it would be well for those with younger children to keep them in mind. If they do, perhaps their children will not be among those who run away to find a home.

Learn to Listen. Runaways told Dr. Peale again and again that parents don't listen. He suggested that parents let what was once almost a monologue—the parents'—become a dialogue. Even when you don't agree with your teen-ager, listen to him and be sure that he knows that you are listening.

Don't Try to Make Your Child Into a Carbon Copy of Yourself. Dr. Peale feels that too many parents expect their children to have the same interests and preferences that they have. Recognize your child's individuality.

Give Explanations. Explain the whys and wherefores of your rules and regulations. Because parents supply food, clothing, shelter, and money, they feel that their authority should be absolute and unquestioned. But Dr. Peale observes that adolescents are quickly alienated when they are made to feel that they are just objects to be ordered about.

Don't Be a Pushover. Young people do not respect spineless parents. It breeds not only contempt in children but also a feeling of insecurity. Even as youths rebel against authority and demand the right to speak for themselves, most desire and need a framework of discipline. They may want more freedom, but total freedom frightens them.

Parents show they care when they use loving, reasonable discipline.

Remember to Apologize to Your Children Sometimes. If you find that you made a mistake, tell your child that you are sorry.

Examine Your Own Lives. Parents should keep a careful watch over themselves. Dr. Peale noted that much of the disillusionment of runaways results from observing the difference between what parents teach and how they conduct themselves. They teach high ideals, but don't live up to them.

Dr. Peale's conclusion was that young people are not likely to run away from parents they admire or from a home where they feel loved.

---

[1] Paul Tournier, M.D., *Escape From Loneliness* (Philadelphia: The Westminster Press, 1962), pp. 133, 134.

[2] Joan B. Kelly and Judith S. Walterslein, "How Schools Can Help the Children of Divorce," *National Elementary Principal,* October, 1979, pp. 51-58.

Eyes That See, Ears That Hear

*T*he students saluted the flag, sang the national anthem, and then Teacher took the attendance record. "Now, boys and girls," I said to my pupils, "let's talk about what you saw on the way to school this morning."

A hush descended on the classroom. This was a new idea. What *had* they seen on the way to school?

"Tom, you ride the bus. As you looked out the windows, what did you see?"

"I don't know," Tom shrugged with a sheepish grin.

"Mary, as you walked down the street this morning, what did you see?"

The little girl thought hard. She could think of nothing she had seen.

"Mary, you walked past many houses. You passed yards where trees were growing, where flowers were blooming, where cars were parked, where dogs were barking. Think about what you saw."

After this introduction of interesting possibilities, when this question was asked on other mornings the children could tell many things they had seen on the way to school or on the way home. They began to look at the world with seeing eyes.

One morning a different question was posed. "Let's talk about what you heard on the way to school."

The hush descended again. What *had* they heard on the way to school? What about the sound of wind in the trees, of rain splashing on sidewalks, of machinery, or of living creatures of the earth? There was much for them to hear.

Most of us go through life with slumbering senses, making use of only a small part of our mental resources. As the prophet Ezekiel lamented, in a different context, the people of Israel "have eyes to see, and see not; they have ears to hear, and hear not" (Eze. 12:2).

That all too many of us have eyes and see not was indicated during World War II by experiments at Ohio State University. It was found that Air Force applicants were using their eyes at only about 20 percent of their capacity.

That many of us have ears that hear not was noted by Rachel Carson, the late marine biologist and author. She wrote that people had told her they never heard the song of a wood thrush, although she knew that this bird sang in their yards every spring.

Because their senses are only half awake, most people reach only half of their learning potential. All that we learn we apprehend through five channels of communication—seeing, hearing, smelling, tasting, and touching. Of the five senses, a high percentage of what we know was learned through seeing, a small percentage was learned through hearing, and a tiny percentage through the other senses.

It is the responsibility of both the home and the school to help children become skilled in the art of observation, to open their senses to the flora and fauna in their environment—to see, hear, smell, taste, and feel what is about them.

Sometimes inattention in school is the fault of the teacher, because she presents instruction in a dull way. Sometimes it is caused by the children's fatigue, as a result of late hours and overly stimulating television programs. Many times, however, a pupil is inattentive because his senses have not been developed. He does not see or hear what is going on in school.

Once after the school principal interrupted a lesson to give me a message and then left the room, I asked the class, seemingly attentive during the interlude, what color hair Mr. Miles had.

Only a few hands went up.

"What color suit was he wearing?" I asked.

Not many knew.

Although not one of the students had a hearing defect, only about half the class could repeat the principal's message to me, even though it was spoken clearly. It was apparent that unless their senses were sharpened, unless they became alert, they would miss many things going on around them.

When a young nephew stayed with my family for a time, we played games that helped him learn to take notice.

"Let's go out into the world," I would say to him, "and see what we can see." We went out into the streets of the neighborhood.

"I see a cat on a fence," I would say. "What do you see?"

"I see a car in a garage. What do you see?"

"I see the streak of a jet."

"I see a boy on a bicycle."

Sometimes we went outdoors to listen.

"I hear the buzzing of a bee. What do you hear?"

"I hear the barking of a dog. What do you hear?"

"I hear the honking of a horn."

"I hear someone playing the piano."

Sometimes in the evening we went out into the back yard to hear nighttime voices—crickets chirping, frogs croaking, tiny creatures fiddling.

At times we explored the world through our other senses, and these experiences proved to be as inspiring and delightful as seeing and hearing.

Stimulate the sensory capacity of your child by playing with him such games as touch and tell, and smell and tell. Sometimes blindfold him and hand him familiar objects, seeing how many he can identify by feel. While he is blindfolded, give him objects to smell. How many can he identify by odor? The first few times you play this game you probably will be startled at how few of the objects he recognizes, even though they are part of his daily life.

After a visitor has been in your home when your son or daughter was present, ask the child to describe her appearance. What color are her eyes and hair? What color were her dress and shoes? How much of the conversation can he recall? Such activities will help to sharpen the child's senses, make him skilled in observation, more aware of activities going on.

One spring evening the authoress Michael Drury was walking down a New York street with a friend, a man who was weighted with problems. Suddenly he stopped and said, "I hear a cricket." In the midst of blowing horns, roaring traffic, and chattering crowds he heard one of nature's voices. They searched for the creature and found it perched on a grating. How few people have senses so keenly tuned to their surroundings.

All about us are sights, sounds, colors, shapes, and smells. How dimly we are aware of them. How little we do to help children develop awareness.

Helen Keller, blind and deaf from infancy, advised people with seeing eyes and ears, "Use your eyes as if tomorrow you would be stricken blind." She told them to hear the sounds about them "as if you would be stricken deaf tomorrow." "Make the most of every sense: glory in all the facets of pleasure and beauty which the world reveals to you."

We might add, Help your children make the most of their senses. Then when they look out at the world they will have eyes that see and ears that hear.

Help Your Child to Wonder

*L*et's go out and look at the stars," my mother said to me one summer evening when I was about 5 years old. We went out of the lamplighted farmhouse, across the clover-scented yard, and stood beside the barbed-wire fence that marked the boundary between our farm and the neighbor's. As we looked up into the heavens Mother made no attempt to name the heavenly bodies; in fact, I do not remember that any words were spoken as we stood there.

We were filled with awe at the majesty of the heavens, at the myriad lights, at the wispy streak of the Milky Way, at the bright, clear patterns of the constellations, at an occasional meteor that blazed its way into the earth's atmosphere.

After a while we returned to the lamplight, I to go to bed and Mother to do her mending. Neither of us realized at the time that my mind had photographed the starlit scene and that I would always remember the child and her mother, one midsummer night, pondering together the mystery and the immensity of the universe.

Mother had little to give her children in the way of material gifts, but she gave us something more meaningful than anything that might have been wrapped in paper or tied with ribbon. Her imperishable gift was appreciation of beauty, a sense of wonder at the exquisite handiwork of God revealed in nature. Too few parents today take time to share with their children moments of beauty—a rainbow, a rosebud, a sunset—to explore the marvels and mysteries of their natural surroundings.

Arthur Gordon, in an article in *Guideposts* (June, 1966),

related a moment of wonder that he as a small boy had shared with his father. It was an experience that changed the world of his childhood.

The Gordons lived by the sea, in a tall house with a peaked roof so high that it rose above all the surrounding houses. Near the top of the roof was a trapdoor that could be reached only by propping a ladder on the attic floor. Consequently no one ever climbed up there.

One sunny day when Arthur and his father were in the attic, Mr. Gordon looked up at the trapdoor. "It must be a real view from up there. Let's take a look."

Arthur felt excited and also fearful as he started up the ladder, his father right behind him.

They climbed until Arthur's head touched the trapdoor. Then his father unhooked the latch and slid the door back. From the protective circle of his father's arm the boy looked out at a world he had never seen before.

The sea stretched to the horizon, so expansive and gigantic that it seemed to reach into infinity. Below him lay the tops of houses—and the backs of sea gulls as they passed in flight. The well-known path through the dunes was a winding thread shimmering in the sunlight. The world he looked at was so immense, its horizons so drastically changed, that for him it had been forever altered.

When Gordon wrote the article, his father had been dead many years. And yet the rooftop experience remained as vivid in memory as though it had happened the previous day. He stated that he often remembered it on Father's Day—just as he remembered other warm, shared experiences with his dad.

All young children have a sense of wonder. Invariably in my classroom when we would talk about natural phenomena—the sun, the moon, the stars—a hush would descend; even the noisiest pupils became quiet. Parents and teachers have the responsibility of keeping alive this sense of awe, of stimulating and extending it, developing an appreciation for the handiwork of God.

Rachel Carson wrote that when the moon was full the family would let her nephew, Roger, stay up past his bedtime. He would join them beside the picture window in the unlighted living room and watch the moon sink "lower and lower toward the far side of the bay." As it sank, the water blazed with silver flames. Miss Carson thought that the memory of such a scene would be more meaningful to Roger in his future years than the sleep he had lost.

During the daylight hours she and Roger would explore their natural environment. Sometimes the exploration took them to "a world of seaweed and fishes and creatures of bizarre shape and habit, of tides rising and falling on their appointed schedule, of exposed mud flats and salt rime drying on the rocks."

Sometimes they explored the woodland, on the alert for a fox or a deer. Surrounded by spruce trees, they would play their "Christmas tree" game, choosing trees for the various creatures of the woods. The finger-size seedlings were for the little bugs, the saplings were for the rabbits and the woodchucks, and the big trees were for the deer and the moose.

For many families it is not possible to adventure at the ocean or in a woodland, but there are other ways to share and enjoy the wonders of nature.

A flowerpot, some soil, and a bulb will produce a miracle—a daffodil, a narcissus, or a tulip.

A bowl of fish is a bowl of wonder to a child. He can spend happy moments watching the colorful creatures dart about in the water.

A bay window can become a flower garden ablaze with geraniums and marigolds.

Your back yard can be a natural wonderland. At night take a flashlight and go out with your child to the garden. Listen to nighttime voices—croaking frogs, chirping crickets, and singing insects.

To help your child explore the marvels and mysteries of his environment, give him gifts that stimulate and extend the sense of wonder he was born with, gifts that keep alive in him a sensitive appreciation of beauty. Instead of giving him a toy gun or other toy weapons, which would build up in him a feeling of violence and hostility, give him a magnifying glass, a microscope, binoculars.

As he examines a blossom through the magnifying glass, he sees beauty and perfection in all its parts.

As he peers at a drop of pond water through the microscope,

he sees ordinarily invisible multitudes. A microscope will open to him a world he scarcely knew existed.

With binoculars he can see birds close up and distinguish their colors and markings.

Give him a telescope to permit him to explore the innumerable stars suspended in space.

Give him seeds, bulbs, garden tools, a book of gardening instructions.

Lesley Frost, daughter of the poet Robert Frost, said of her childhood: "We were very poor—only we didn't realize it then. We didn't have a piano, but we had books. We didn't have chemistry sets or dissecting sets, but we had science lessons—astronomy, botany, and the greatest of lessons from nature. We had a telescope to help us study the stars. What more, really, could a child ask?"

There is one more thing for which a child could ask: some of his parents' time, time so that they might go out together and look at the stars, at a rainbow, a sunset.

"He who tarries to look at a sunset," wrote a wise man, "stands very close to God."

Stand close to God with your child.

With a Giant's Step

An educator once said, "The child who early in life learns to depend upon reading as a major source of pleasure walks the world with a giant's step."

Although most parents hope their children will be among those who tread "with a giant's step," few are aware that they as parents play a major role in the development of reading interests. Few realize that it is in the preschool years, the years of golden opportunity for parents, that the seeds of reading success are sown.

Before the child enters school to receive formal instruction, he will have developed certain attitudes toward reading. These will have been conditioned by his home environment.

Tragically there are homes without books, homes in which no one does any reading, homes where the children never have their questionings answered or stories read to them. Children from such homes are to be pitied. They begin school disadvantaged.

Then there are homes in which there are many books, where reading is an essential part of life. Children in these homes are fortunate. They begin school as "head start" children. This is true because almost invariably parents pass on to their offspring their enthusiasm for reading. Young children are imitative. They do what they see their parents and older siblings doing. Thus they learn.

If a child asks, "Why is the sky blue?" and parent and child find in a book the answer to the question, that child begins to recognize reading as a way to find answers.

Children who have parents who take time to read stories to

them are being favorably conditioned toward reading. Not only will the child be flattered by the parent's undivided attention, he will also be emotionally reassured. Natural pleasures will be associated with books.

An editorial in the *Saturday Review* stated, "All parents would do well to remember that preparation for college boards begins when they start reading to their preschool children."

Talking records may be purchased that read stories to the child. These may have a place in times of illness when the child is confined to bed and the mother's time is limited, but an impersonal, unknown voice, mechanically transmitted, should be used only at exceptional times.

Writer Lesley Conger has this to say about the way a book should be read to a child:

"A book should be read to a child with love, with a warm lap, with encircling arms, with a kiss now and then on top of the head. A book should be read in the cozy engulfment of a deep armchair, in a rocker, in bed, or on the rug in front of the fireplace, flat on stomachs side by side, heads together. A book should be read by a truly human voice, a motherly voice, a fatherly voice, the voice of an indulgent auntie or an obliging uncle, a grandma's voice . . . the voice of a sister or brother." [1]

While you are sitting close to your child, reading to him, allow him to turn the pages. Take time for him to look at the pictures, to ask questions about what you are reading. Never discourage questions in a child. It is the way he enlarges his horizons. It is the way he reaches out to explore the world. And when he asks you to read what signs and labels say—on a loaf of bread, on a can of soup, or on a bar of soap—do so. These are all prereading experiences. From these brief, informal contacts with the printed word, much learning takes place.

Elizabeth Borton de Treviño, who was awarded the John Newbery Medal for having written the most distinguished book for young people in 1966—*I, Juan de Pareja*—mentioned in her acceptance speech a number of people who, she felt, had had a part in the award. At the top of the list she placed her parents, who had early instilled in her a love for books.

The Franklin Roosevelt family had an interesting tradition

associated with books. Every Christmas Eve the President would read a portion of Dickens' *Christmas Carol* to his children and his children's children. Probably as long as these family members live they will remember with nostalgia the closeness and the warmth of those occasions when Grandfather Roosevelt read to them about the true meaning of Christmas.

In earlier years in America, when religion was more deeply rooted in the homelife than it is today, there were family traditions associated with the reading of the Bible. In the morning and evening in many homes the family would gather together in the parlor or sit around a table while Father would read portions of the Scriptures.

"Study not the philosophy of man's conjectures, but study the philosophy of Him who is truth. No other literature can compare with this in value."—*The Ministry of Healing,* pp. 459, 460.

Counseling parents with respect to reading the Scriptures to their children, Ellen G. White stated: "Reverently and tenderly let the word of God be read and repeated to them in portions suited to their comprehension and adapted to awaken their interest."—*Ibid.,* p. 460.

One of the most unfortunate aspects of modern family life is that there is so little time given to such meaningful, shared experiences. Too many of today's parents find it easier to give their children material things—the latest car, a color television set—than to give of themselves. And yet it is in the giving of time and attention that families are bound together and life's true values are developed.

Edith F. Hunter wrote: "Rich, varied, first-handed experience, reinforced and broadened by reading, is the best education that children can have. Such experience does not require great wealth or even highly educated parents. . . . Certainly one of the chief ingredients in the education of our children is the books we are enjoying together. . . . The stories we have read together I know have strengthened the fabric of our life as a family." [2]

To expose children to the right kind of books is a parental responsibility, and it should be shared by teachers and librarians. This should be taken as seriously as other matters that concern child welfare. Sometimes parents who are concerned about the nutrition and physical health of their children are unconcerned about the nourishment of the young mind. All too often this area of development is left to chance, with unfortunate results. The impressionable, inquiring mind of the child is fed with comics, tawdry television programs, and the distorted illustrations and puerile texts of cheap and inferior books.

"Never should books containing a perversion of truth be placed in the hands of children or youth. Let not our children, in the very process of obtaining an education, receive ideas that will prove to be seeds of sin. If those with mature minds had nothing to do with such books, they would themselves be far safer, and their example and influence on the right side would make it far less difficult to guard the youth from temptation.

"We have an abundance of that which is real, that which is divine. Those who thirst for knowledge need not go to polluted fountains."—*The Ministry of Healing,* p. 447.

During the impressionable years the child should be introduced to books that have strength, vitality, and beauty, books that not only delight the mind but build character, books that foster love, compassion, courage, understanding, and idealism.

Biographies of persons who have lived noble, achieving lives are particularly educational and inspirational. It is doubtful that any young person could read the life story of Albert Schweitzer, the great humanitarian, and not have his sense of values affected. Nor could he read about other self-sacrificing people and not be influenced. Each book a child reads becomes a part of him.

Parents are sometimes uncertain as to what books they should select as gifts for their children with respect to age levels and interests. Church school teachers and religious bookstores are always willing to make suggestions when their opinions are solicited. Religious publishers have made available inspirational books for all age groups.

It is well to have a special place for a child to keep his books. If a bookcase is not available, one can be made from orange crates or other boxes. Shelves can be built in them, and they can be made attractive with paint or paper. A place of his own for the books that are his own will encourage a child's interest and will stimulate him to begin collecting favorite books.

Parents do well to give time and attention to the developing of reading interests. As they guide their children into meaningful reading experiences they will help them to reading success—to walk the world "with a giant's step."

---

[1] Reprinted by permission from *The Writer*. Copyright © 1966 by The Writer, Inc.
[2] From "The Peace of Great Books" by Edith F. Hunter, The Horn Book Magazine, December, 1964. Copyright © 1964 by the Horn Book, Inc.

"Love Me, Mommy!"

Jon told the college counselor that one of his most vivid memories was of an experience he had as a young child. He had unintentionally broken an object that was treasured by his mother, and she had upbraided him harshly. Crushed by her verbal abuse, he had run to her, thrown his arms around her, and sobbed, "Love me, Mommy!"

But Mommy hadn't loved him. She had angrily unwound his arms, thrust him from her, and stormed out of the room.

During childhood Jon was often denounced when his mother's wrath was aroused over trifling offenses. However, he would no longer sob, "Love me, Mommy!" It wouldn't have done any good. He stoically came to accept her angry denunciations and to expect neither forgiveness nor acceptance.

Now he was a college student, ill at ease with himself and with others. Disquieted by emotional problems, he had sought the help of the counselor.

Too few parents realize that it is during infancy and childhood, as the child interacts with the important people in his life, that the foundation for mental health is laid. It is within the context of the family that he is emotionally and psychologically nourished. The words, the acts, and the deportment of the parents—even the expressions on their faces—influence the attitudes of those within the home. It is within this context that a child feels either loved or unloved, accepted or rejected, fearful or confident, worthy or unworthy. It is these cumulative attitudes that help him to experience victory or defeat in his later confrontation with life.

One of the most common emotional ailments treated by

counselors is a feeling of worthlessness, a lack of self-esteem. This is particularly unfortunate because a sense of self-worth is a basic psychological and emotional need. This is not to be equated with self-centeredness or a feeling of superiority. Self-centeredness and ego-serving sow the seeds for poor mental health just as surely as do pronounced feelings of helplessness and hopelessness. Jesus knew that egocentricity was self-destructive. This is why He counseled: "If any man will come after me, let him deny himself" (Matt. 16:24).

A healthy sense of self-worth involves a genuine acceptance of self. It means believing in oneself and having confidence in one's ability to function adequately.

Cora was a young person who did not believe in herself. She had been referred to the counseling center by a friend who had noted her marked depression.

When Roger Dudley, a director of guidance and counseling, invited her into his office, she told him, " 'I can't eat. I can't sleep. I can't study. I'm failing in school. I'm jittery. I'm not getting along with people. . . . I'm a wreck.' "

The story she told Roger was one that is often repeated to counselors. "She felt worthless," Roger wrote in an *Adventist Review* article entitled "The Family—Seedbed for Mental Health." "Not only did she dislike herself; she did not see how anybody else could like her either. She had very little confidence in her ability to do anything right." *

Over a period of weeks Roger helped Cora to develop self-confidence, to be aware that she was a person of intrinsic worth.

Because a person's basic feelings about himself help to determine his mental health—and his behavioral responses—it is important for parents to know how to help children develop a sense of self-esteem. Here are some suggestions to keep in mind and some approaches to use in reaching this most vital objective.

Don't put tags on your children. It's fine to label the packages in the freezer, but don't put negative labels on your children. Young children have a natural inclination to believe what important people in their lives tell them. When their parents tell them that they are lazy, clumsy, or dull, they incorporate these messages into part of their self-image.

Many parents unintentionally give their children ego-damaging messages. In so doing they undermine their sense of personal adequacy. Avoid labeling your children in ways such as these:

"Don't forget to bring home your reader, Nellie. You're a poor reader and you need extra practice." The more often you remind Nellie that she's a poor reader, the longer she'll remain one. She'll accept your appraisal.

"Eat your potatoes, Mary. You're so skinny now we can hardly see you." Such remarks will make Mary self-conscious about her appearance.

"Mrs. Smith, this is Tom, our youngest child. He's our bashful boy." Calling attention to Tom's introversion won't help to extrovert him. It will only deepen his shyness. An introduction such as the following would be better:

"This is Tom, our youngest child. He's the family puzzle whiz. You should see some of the puzzles he puts together." By calling attention to an area in which he excels, you encourage self-confidence.

Accent the positive. There are other areas in which positive approaches help to influence children toward feelings of adequacy.

When a child brings home corrected papers from school, try to find something positive to commend before you pounce on the mistakes. For example:

"This is very nice writing, Jane. I'm glad you take time to work carefully. And it's a neat paper. I'm glad it doesn't have a lot of erasures and scratch-outs.

"I see that the teacher marked five of these problems wrong. After we do the dishes this evening, I'll help you. We'll find out what you didn't understand. Then next time you'll do better."

It doesn't take a psychiatrist to see that this approach is far more nurturing to the child's self-esteem than the following:

"You missed five problems. What in the world is wrong with you? Why don't you keep your mind on your work? I'm ashamed of you!"

If you were the child, which of these approaches would you

prefer? Which one would encourage you to try harder and to do better? Wouldn't it be the approach that commended you for what you did well and offered help with what you did incorrectly? Wouldn't your heart be chilled by the approach that was censorious and belittling?

Don't play favorites. Parents should be particularly careful not to adopt a demeaning attitude toward their less-attractive, less-capable children. Under no circumstances should partiality be manifested or favoritism shown. To favor the personable and academically gifted child and to nag and criticize the less favored are forms of child abuse.

Danny is a tragic example of a youth who was abused through demeaning. But it doesn't hurt him anymore.

Eighteen-year-old Danny had suffered epileptic seizures for ten years. Unfortunately he was also intellectually limited. His grades were below average and he dropped out of school after his junior year in high school. Later he enrolled in a school that offered a vocational rehabilitation program.

Adjustment at the new school was difficult. A mentally slow, seizure-prone youth does not make friends easily. Danny found no acceptance from his peers—not even from the school counselor.

Had Danny found warmth at home, the rejection at school would have been tempered. But his father ridiculed him, and an older sister quarreled with him. The stress brought on more seizures. Crushed by failure at school and rejection at home, Danny hung himself shortly before Christmas.

"No matter how hard he tried," said Dr. David L. Coulter, of the University of Michigan Medical Center, "he could never succeed in school, and other children ridiculed his failure." Danny could find no area of personal accomplishment, nothing that could provide him with a sense of worth. His classmates ridiculed him for having seizures, and his family considered him worthless because of his epilepsy.

The environment in which Danny was reared prepared him for failure. He had too few experiences with success and too many with frustrations and feelings of inadequacy.

Physically unattractive and slow-learning children are particularly in need of encouragement and sympathy. No one can remain emotionally and psychologically healthy if he is frequently demeaned by those who are important to him. His self-confidence will be eroded, and a growing sense of inadequacy will cause him to give up.

It is important for parents to structure experiences so that each child in the family will have some success, an area of personal accomplishment that will provide him with a sense of worth, an area that will receive approval from others.

Let them know you care. Parents should let their children know that they care for them. An article in *Have a Good Day,* published by Tyndale House, is entitled "Have You Hugged Your Dog Today?" An even better article and title would be "Have You Hugged Your Child Today?" There are people who remember to give their pets pats of approval but do not remember to give their children indications of affection.

One mother said she sometimes tells her 7-year-old son, "If I were to look at a whole catalog of little boys, I would still choose you."

The same woman said to her daughter, age 9, "Your dad and I were just discussing today how fortunate we are to have such beautiful, bright, well-behaved children."

How many children hear words such as these? Or such as the following?

"You're the best son a father could have."

"We are so happy that God sent you to us."

"You are a blessing in our home."

"No matter what happens to you out in the world, we'll always love you."

The awareness of parental love will nurture a feeling of self-worth. Children with this knowledge will never have to run to a parent, cling frantically, and sob beseechingly—and futilely— "Love, me, Mommy." They will know from their earliest years that both Mommy and Daddy love them.

---

*Roger L. Dudley, "The Family—Seedbed for Mental Health," *Adventist Review,* March 27, 1980.

Partners in the Home

*P*robably there is no area of child growth and development that causes more problems and anxieties in the home than that of discipline. Whether or not parents succeed in reaching the true object of discipline (which is to prepare the child for self-government) largely predetermines whether the child will be prepared to meet successfully the stern discipline of life.

Without clearly defined expectations, children do not know whether what they are doing is right or wrong, whether they are succeeding or failing. If a child is given the responsibility to empty the wastebaskets, he knows that when he has emptied them he has done what was expected of him. If he has been told that he is to play in his own yard, he knows that when he obeys, he has done right. Without guidelines the child can know only uncertainty. This is also true when parents are not consistent in the way they enforce their restrictions. If on Monday a child is punished for playing in the street and on Wednesday the same infraction is overlooked, the child becomes confused. He is never sure whether or not his behavior is acceptable. To live in an atmosphere of uncertainty is not conducive to good mental or emotional health. Rather, it creates anxieties.

Research in child development shows that children with high self-esteem and healthy attitudes toward responsibilities usually come from homes where parents clearly define limits and express explicit expectations that they consistently enforce. Interestingly, these are loving, nurturing homes.

It is important to establish love relationships in the home, for the spirit manifested there is the predominant influence in determining behavioral responses in the child. He absorbs what he sees reflected in the behavior and attitudes of his parents. It is through identification with those he loves that the child's most enduring learning takes place.

If a child is aware that in the eyes of his parents he is a valued and loved person, he will be psychologically prepared to learn what they want to teach him. He will be more inclined to act in ways that will please them. On the other hand, if there is contention in the home, if parents are irritable and faultfinding, their children partake of the same spirit. Unwittingly these parents often cause the disciplinary problems that arise. The relationship between them and their children is that of antagonists.

One way to prepare children psychologically to be responsive to parental guidance is to make them feel that they are partners in the home. Even very young children should be given responsibilities and made to feel that their help is needed and appreciated.

One afternoon while I was supervising older children on the playground, a first-grade boy hurried across the yard. The primary school had been dismissed, and he was going to his home across the street. When he neared me I spoke to him, but he didn't seem interested in conversation.

"My daddy is away," he explained gravely, "and I have to hurry home. I promised him that I would take care of my mother."

This child had been made to feel that he was a partner in the home and that his help was needed. He was aware that his parents had confidence in him and considered him able to accept responsibility. He responded to their trust.

Another example of similar parental wisdom comes to mind. One day while I was visiting at a home, the father decided to wash his car. He got a bucket and cleaning cloths for himself, and a smaller bucket and cloth for his 4-year-old son. The boy was assigned a part of the car to wash. The youngster took his assignment seriously. He would stop at times to see how Daddy was doing. Then he would resume his work and try hard to do it just as Daddy did. When the task was finished, the child was thanked for his help and commended on the fine job he had done. He was made to feel that his help was meaningful and appreciated.

In assigning tasks to children, parents should be careful that the assignments are in keeping with the child's age and ability. I was dismayed once at a mother's overexpectations of a 6-year-old.

"A load of wood had been dumped in the yard," she said, "and I told Ron to stack it against the side of the house. When he finished, I went out to see how he had done. Some of the wood was piled right, but some of it was out of line. I knocked it all down and told him to start over."

Ron started over, and once again he came to tell his mother he had finished. Once again she went to inspect his work.

"Some of it still wasn't piled right," she said, "so I knocked it down again. He has to learn to do his work right."

This mother was demanding from a young child the kind of performance that she might have expected from an adult. It is not surprising that Ron became a child with problems. Parents who are unrealistic in their expectations discourage children, causing them to feel that they might as well stop trying.

Parents also discourage children when they use harsh and condemnatory disciplinary measures, causing their children to become afraid to tell the truth. This defeats the purpose of discipline, which is to help a child develop a value system, including truthfulness.

In homes where there is a right spirit, parents don't abuse their children either verbally or physically. They temper authority with affection, making their children aware that discipline is administered because they are cared for, not for personal revenge. Wise parents do not correlate their standards of acceptable behavior with the giving or withholding of love.

Sometimes we hear a parent say, "I won't love you if you do this or that."

I once heard a mother tell her child, "The angels won't love you if you don't mind."

There are those who tell children that Jesus won't love them if they break this or that rule. Jesus loves us regardless of our behavior. He hates the sin but loves the sinner. He loved the prodigal son just as much when he was eating husks in a far country as He did when he was in his Father's house. It was because He loved the boy that His arms were outstretched to welcome him back.

43

Instilling in a child the belief that Jesus doesn't love him if he misbehaves can have unfortunate consequences in later years. There may come a time when a young person thus taught leaves his Father's house. There may be a time when he, too, will be eating husks in a far country. If he believes that his sins have forfeited God's love, he will feel there is no hope for him. "God hates sinners. I'm a sinner. Therefore, God rejects me."

The truth is that God loves all sinners and is waiting to welcome them back to the fold. He is waiting to grant them the enabling power to overcome their sins.

"The love of God still yearns over the one who has chosen to separate from Him, and He sets in operation influences to bring him back to the Father's house."—*Christ's Object Lessons,* p. 202.

Parents who rightly represent God to their children will have a forgiving attitude toward the mistakes and errors their little ones make. They will punish them for misbehavior, but they will not remind them at a later time of incidents that should have been forgiven and forgotten. They will teach their children to bring their mistakes to Jesus, to ask His forgiveness.

A mother whose son voluntarily told her about something wrong that he had done at school was asked how she trained her children to be so truthful.

She explained. "From a very early age I tucked each child in his bed at night and asked this question, 'Is there anything you want to tell mother so you can enjoy a good night's sleep?'

"Sometimes little deeds of unkindness would pour from their hearts. After prayer and a remark or two relating to my confidence in them to do better, they looked forward to a good night's rest. I told them many times, 'I may not always know what you do, but remember, God knows. I want your record in heaven to be spotless at the close of each day.' " *

Children who are taught to bring their mistakes to Jesus for forgiveness will not be, in later years, among those whose souls are weighed down by a sense of guilt. They learned at a tender age how to unload their burden of guilt, how a man can be just with God.

In homes where there is a right spirit, parents are not too proud to admit that they too make mistakes. A high school teacher once asked his class to work together on preparing advice they would like to give to their parents. Some of this was on the subject of parental perfection. The students felt no need for perfect parents, feeling that an occasional goof and an admission of it by Mom and Dad only made them seem more human.

A mother sent her 12-year-old son to the store for groceries. When he returned, she checked to see whether he had brought home the right change. Counting hastily, she thought he had withheld some. "Where is the money?" she stormed. "I will not have a thief for a son."

Patiently the boy checked the purchases with her and proved that he had given her the right change.

Did she apologize? No. She was too ego-centered to admit that she had made a mistake, but brushed the matter aside without an apology.

The father of two sons also made a mistake. He handled it in a different manner.

One day, believing his 5-year-old son was guilty of serious misbehavior, he spanked the child hard. Later he learned that the boy's younger brother was guilty of the misdeed. Dismayed at his error, the father took the wronged child on his lap and told him he was sorry for the mistake he had made. "Please forgive me," he said.

"I already have," the child answered quickly.

Which of the two homes showed a right spirit? In which would the child feel kindly toward his parent? Which best exemplified Christian parenthood?

There is another aspect of parent-child relationships that conditions children to be responsive to parental guidance. There is better rapport in homes where parents treat their children as individuals and not as "things." Such parents encourage children to use their reasoning powers. Father and mother listen to their thoughts and show respect for their ideas. They want their children to be thinkers "and not mere reflectors of other men's thought" (*Education,* p. 17). They are aware that only as a child develops his powers of reasoning and judgment will he be prepared, at a later time, to resist pressures toward group conformity.

45

Children who are controlled by harsh discipline, forced into subjection through fear or force, will have weak mental and moral powers. With their mind and will under the complete control of parents, they may never learn to exercise their power of reasoning. Trained like animals, when they leave home and are away from the pull of the halter, they will not know how to think or act or judge for themselves. Consequently they will be incapable of discerning between truth and error, and will be an easy prey to deception.

"A child may be so trained as to have . . . no will of his own. Even his individuality may be merged in the one who superintends his training. . . . [Children] have not been taught to move from reason and principle; their wills have been controlled by another, and the mind has not been called out, that it might expand and strengthen by exercise."—*Child Guidance,* pp. 210, 211.

It is important for parents to be united in the discipline of their children. Sometimes one parent is indulgent and inclined to overlook disobedience, while the other is firm and expects obedience. If they work at cross-purposes the child will not be sure what is expected of him. In all probability he will turn to the permissive parent for his directives. This can cause rifts. Although no parent should permit a child to be abused, they should, in normal circumstances, support each other in the discipline that is meted. If there are differences of opinion, these should be discussed when the child is not present.

* Ruth McLin and Jeanne Larson, *Creative Ideas for Child Training* (Washington, D.C.: Review and Herald Pub. Assn., 1973), p. 109.

What Would Daddy Do?

*I*n an article in the June, 1980, issue of *Decision,* Allen C. Emery, Jr., wrote: "Today I still ask myself, What would Daddy do? with those decisions in business and life that are so often not black or white, but gray. I am in debt to the memory-making efforts that my father made to imprint indelibly upon my mind the meaning of integrity."

Emery remembered rides that he and his father had taken on the train to Boston. At times the conductor would neglect to take their tickets. But this did not result in a loss to the railroad. Mr. Emery never left the train without first giving the conductor the tickets.

Emery also remembered the time his father purchased an expensive pair of German binoculars. The glasses were lost, and Mr. Emery reported it to the insurance company and received a check for replacement. A year later the binoculars were found, and on that same day he wrote a letter to the insurers and enclosed a check for the amount they had sent him.*

Although Mr. Emery responded in honorable ways because of deeply ingrained personal integrity, he probably was aware, also, that parents are to be correct models to their children, setting examples of the strictest integrity. He was aware that what little eyes see and little ears hear make an imprint upon tender minds and that no aftercircumstances of life can entirely erase such impressions. Because Mr. Emery had this awareness, his son, in later years, faced the decisions of life with the certain answer to the question What would Daddy do? Daddy would do whatever represented honor and integrity. Because of this, his son would do likewise.

Another father also showed unusual integrity. One time the family went to a resort. Some maps lay on the counter, and because maps were usually free, the father assumed that those were and took one. After reaching home, he became aware that the price was twenty-five cents. The family immediately returned to the resort, a distance of thirty miles, and Dad paid for the map.

"Undeviating principle should govern parents in all the affairs of life, especially in the education and training of their children." "Honesty should stamp every action of our lives."—*Child Guidance,* pp. 151, 154.

Not many children are blessed with parents who have honesty stamped on every action of their lives. Eight-year-old Marian didn't have this kind of parent. One day at school she said to me, "I was in the store with my mother. She opened her purse and put in a pair of socks. She didn't pay for them. She does that a lot of times."

A certain teen-age girl didn't have an honest parent either. Allen Emery wrote about her in his article about his father. She was a member of their Bible club. One day she rang their doorbell. It was evident that she had been crying, and after being seated she wept again. "Mother wants me to tell a lie," she sobbed. She told them that her mother had asked her to tell the neighbors that her new coat had been purchased at Filene's, although she had actually bought it at the Bargain Center. Her mother had even sewed a Filene label into the garment. "It would be a lie," the girl wept. "She told me I must tell a lie." *

Then there was the mother of a son who had taken a pen out of a classmate's purse. When the teacher asked her to come to school to discuss the theft, the mother said, "My son tells me everything, and he says he was joking with the pen. Why would he steal a pen? It's ridiculous. He doesn't need a pen. Why, he has all the pens he can use. Just last week I took him a handful of pens from the office where I work, so he doesn't have to steal one."

The unfortunate children of these parents were affected or misdirected by wrong home influences, by the deceptive practices of their parents. They will carry the memories of these wrong deeds with them through life. And it may well be that when a time of temptation comes to them—to lie, to steal, to cheat—they will respond in the way they remember that their parents responded.

Wrong parental example destroys the child's confidence in his parents. A pastor once said that he observed the youth who left the church. In 65 to 70 percent of the dropouts, he found that the child had first lost confidence in his parents, followed by distrust of the church. If religion had done nothing for his parents, what could it do for him? This minister and his wife found that the only way they could gain the confidence of their children was to be completely honest in all their dealings.

In his article on runaways, mentioned in a previous chapter, Norman Vincent Peale counseled parents to examine their lives. In his talks with many runaway children, he had observed that much of their disillusionment was the result of their awareness of the difference between what their parents said and how they lived. "They tell you to have high ideals, but they break every commandment in the book" was a common reaction.

"It is because so many parents and teachers profess to believe the Word of God while their lives deny its power, that the teaching of Scripture has no greater effect upon the youth."—*Child Guidance,* p. 218.

It is a sobering thought for parents to remember that long after they are at rest in their graves, their lives will live on in the lives of their children—and in the lives of their children's children. These offspring will bear, in some way and to some extent, the imprint of parental influence. This is the legacy of parenthood.

Fortunate are the children who remember consistent examples of parental honor and integrity. Fortunate are those who can say in later years when confronted by temptation to do wrong, "I know what Mother would do. I know what Daddy would do. *And* I know what I shall do. I shall have no part in this wrongdoing."

---

* Allen C. Emery, "What Would Daddy Do?" *Decision,* June, 1980.

Diet and Schoolchildren

Mary Lou, a beautiful teen-ager, was rushed to the hospital emergency room, suffering from acute appendicitis. Surgery was performed, but problems ensued. Because her abdominal muscles lacked strength and tone, the incision was closed with considerable difficulty. It opened in a few hours. There were repeated unsuccessful attempts at closure. Ordinarily, recovery in a patient this young would have occurred in a few days. However, it was several months before Mary Lou's surgery healed.

A study of the patient's case revealed that the problem was caused by malnutrition. For two years Mary Lou's diet had consisted largely of colas and hot dogs.

Although this is an extreme example of dietary abuse, there are large numbers of children and youth who are eating unhealthfully and reaping the consequences. Wrong eating habits are largely responsible for the obesity, anemia, and poor dental health that are widespread among the young.

Ask any dentist how many cavities he is finding in his young patients' teeth. His answer will shock you. An informed dentist will confirm that tooth decay is primarily a school-age disease. Ninety-eight percent of school-age children will suffer from untreated caries by the time they reach 15.

Among children ages 11 to 14 who were screened in Know Your Body programs in the United States during the past several years, it was found that—

35 percent had high cholesterol levels.

20 percent scored fair or poor on an exercise test of cardiac

response.

15 percent were overweight.

40 percent had one or more risk factors for cardiovascular disease.[1]

The poor health found among many youth is not surprising when one considers the fact that more than half the food consumed by the average American each year is junk.

According to Michael Lasky, writing in the March, 1979, issue of *Campus Life,* in a recent year the average American consumed the following:

100 pounds of refined sugar.

55 pounds of fats and oils.

300 cans or bottles of soda.

more than 100 sticks of chewing gum.

more than 20 gallons of ice cream.

18 pounds of candy.

5 pounds of potato chips.

a conservatively estimated 50 pounds of cookies and cakes.

In the first chapter mention was made of Floyd, a second-grade pupil whose mother busied herself with so many social activities that she had no time for her children. Floyd, a disrupter and poor achiever, often came to school without a proper breakfast. His mother was either unaware or did not care that her son's breakfast should have been his most substantial meal of the day. From one third to one half of his day's total supply of needed nutrients should have been provided by his morning meal. This would have supplied him the necessary energy to face the demands of the day, giving him the good start that he and all children need.

Probably, Floyd's mother was also unaware that her child's dietary indiscretions—as a result of her neglect—bore a direct relationship to his aggressive behavior and poor academic achievement. Many other parents are also unaware of this relationship. The highly processed convenience foods and the high-sugar-content foods that some mothers feed their families contribute to the low grades and deviant behavior they decry. There are times when it is not the child who needs a scolding for poor grades or uncooperative behavior. Rather, it is his parents, for they overlook the fact that wrong habits of eating and drinking are a cause of wrong thinking and acting.

"Whatever injures the health, not only lessens physical vigor, but tends to weaken the mental and moral powers."—*The Ministry of Healing,* p. 128. Because the nerves of the brain are disturbed by the abuse heaped on the stomach, persons who eat and drink improperly are often irritable, impatient, and hard to get along with.

The effects of improper eating are markedly indicated on the day following Halloween. Many teachers have noted the antisocial behavior caused by sugar in the bloodstream of the trick-or-treaters. The day after Halloween is often a day of problems at school. Dr. Alan C. Lenin, director of the New York Institute for Child Development, agrees with this. He stated that his office was chaotic on November 1. The students, hyperactive and learning disabled to begin with, had shorter-than-usual attention spans and could not participate in the therapy sessions. Some were almost unmanageable.[2]

A Radford University professor learned the harmfulness of giving his child high-sugar-content foods. "We have taken our son off sugarcoated cereals," he said. "He is much calmer now and getting along much better."[3] Perhaps one he removed from his son's diet was the cereal that claims to be nutritious and to have many vitamins, but in actuality is more than 50 percent sugar.

An increasing number of scientists and doctors are concluding that the junk foods that people eat are a source of antisocial behavior. They are confirming that malnutrition and other nutritional deficiencies can trigger aggressive behavior.

Benjamin Feingold, a physician at Kaiser Permanente in San Francisco, believes that marked changes can be made in pupil behavior and achievement through proper diet. "When synthetic food coloring and flavoring are eliminated from patients' diets," he said, "remarkable personality and behavioral changes occur. Hyperactive children become calmer and more responsive, have a longer attention span, and are better able to cope with their environment. These changes are followed by an improvement in scholastic achievement."[4]

Dr. Herald A. Habenicht agrees with Dr. Feingold. In an article in the May, 1977, issue of *Listen* magazine, he wrote that his practice of pediatric allergy constantly showed him the effects of food coloring, additives, and salicylates. He reported that they caused hyperactivity and behavior and learning problems.

Although educators, like medical doctors, have been slow to recognize the direct relationship between diet and behavior and academic achievement, they are increasingly aware of the relationship. More and more schools are making changes in the food served in their cafeterias. Many are getting rid of machines that dispense junk food.

When the Gilroy, California, school district banned junk-food sales on all nine school campuses, affecting 5,700 pupils, Superintendent Vance Baldwin said he made the decision after concluding there is "strong evidence linking behavior, attitudes, and achievement to a high sugar diet." He said this kind of diet "leads to obesity, mental disease, learning disabilities and diabetes." [5]

Much of the sugar that is consumed by young people is in the large quantities of pop they drink. When a survey was made of food preferences of students in grades 7 to 12, soda pop headed the list of most popular foods.

And what is the content of the average bottle of soft drink? Water. Sugar. Artificial color and artificial flavor. Acid. Some contain harmful substances such as caffeine, theobromine, and phosphoric acid. There is more than half as much caffeine in a twelve-ounce can of cola as there is in a cup of instant coffee.

Pediatricians are becoming increasingly concerned about possible caffeinism in children. Two California dieticians, Mary Bunker and Margaret McWilliams, reporting for the American Dietetic Association, said young people who drink appreciable amounts of cola or chocolate drink may show the effects of the caffeine in irritability, restlessness, nervousness, and sleeplessness. Mrs. Bunker and Mrs. McWilliams explained, "When a very young child drinks a can of cola, the caffeine intake is comparable to an adult drinking four cups of instant coffee." [6]

The sugar content of soft drinks is very high. In fact, the reason that the use of sugar and other sweeteners has climbed steeply in the past ten years is because of the spectacular growth in the consumption of soft drinks. The average bottle of pop contains about one hundred sugar calories per eight ounces.

The action of the sugar and the acid damages the enamel of the teeth. When consumed between meals or just before a meal, the drink takes away the appetite for wholesome food. Thus the body does not get the nutrients essential for health.

Because of the popularity of high-sugar-content foods, enough sugar and other sweeteners are consumed each year to average approximately 120 pounds for every man, woman, and child in the United States. This is about thirty-three teaspoonfuls each day. Most people are not aware of this because the sugar is not eaten by the spoon, but is hidden in foods such as candy, cakes, cookies, pies, doughnuts, ice cream, canned fruits, and, of course, soft drinks.

Why are high-sugar-content foods so popular? The reason is partly because parents condition their children from infancy to have a high regard for sweets. From babyhood sweets are used as pacifiers. When Mother takes Susan to the supermarket and places her in a cart, she hands her a candy bar or a bottle of pop to keep her quiet and occupied. And often at home when a child is upset Mother will get the cookie jar. "Sh! Don't cry! Here's a cookie."

It is often easier for mothers to give their children a cookie or a piece of candy to quiet them than to give the time and attention they need. Sugary pacifiers may answer the purpose for a time, but ultimately they make things worse. When the child's stomach is abused with harmful and unnecessary food the results are often fretfulness, restlessness, and disturbed behavior.

Sweets are often used from early childhood as incentives and for rewards. When Tommy brings home a good report card, he may be rewarded with candy. When Nell has been a good girl she gets a sucker.

My husband and I once visited a State institution for mentally ill persons. One wing of the institution housed emotionally disturbed young people. A teacher explained to us the educational program for these youth. On her desk was a pile of candy bars, and during the discussion she said, "When the children do what they are supposed to do, we give them a candy bar." It was a paradox that educators, sincerely interested in helping the unfortunate youth, would serve them the kind of food that triggered the behavior they were trying to correct. Unfortunately, many parents and other well-meaning adults are also guilty of being "trigger men."

The use of sweets is frequently associated with special and happy occasions. Birthdays mean cake and ice cream—usually heavily frosted cakes. Christmas is associated with sweets. Often there are candy-filled stockings hanging at the fireplace. Peppermint canes often help to decorate the tree. Holidays mean special bakings of cakes, cookies, pies.

There is a constant conditioning of children to the use of high-sugar-content foods. By the time the child is an adult he has become addicted. The addiction is partly based on the fact that sugary foods are pleasing to the taste buds. The more they are eaten, the more they are craved. The addiction is partly psychological, rooted in the fact that the eating of sweets has been associated with pleasurable experiences. And to what has the child become addicted? To food that has empty calories, is a low form of energy, weakens the white blood cells, increases the blood cholesterol, and puts holes in the teeth and pounds on the body. Like other junk food, high-sugar-content foods aggravate aggressive behavior and adversely affect academic achievement.

Persons who think it doesn't matter what kind of food young people eat should consider what Barbara Reed discovered about the relationship between diet and behavior. Barbara, chief probation officer of the Municipal Court of Cuyahoga Falls, Ohio, discovered that juvenile offenders ate large quantities of sugar, soft drinks, and starch. She recommended a sugar-free, low-starch diet and no junk food. The youth who accepted her diet were never back in court. The judge was so impressed with the change in the delinquents that he began to require offenders to eat nutritious diets.[7]

Nutritious diets include whole-grain products, raw fruits and vegetables, nuts (conservatively used), and natural juices.

Unhealthful diets include devitalized white bread with additives, polished white rice, sweetened canned fruits (particularly those canned in heavy syrup), chocolate milk, chemically made ice cream, instant foods, prepared frozen and canned foods that are preserved and doctored with chemical additives—and the high-sugar-content foods already discussed.

Parents should be aware that it is important not only to serve their children nutritious meals but also to eat the same kind of food themselves. An improper and intemperate diet affects the attitudes and temperament of adults, as well as children. It can be a contributing cause of the dissension, strife, unkindness, and impatience that disrupt families and cause children to feel anxious and insecure. This is because the nerves of the brain are adversely affected by the abuse imposed on the stomach.

"Many do not seem to understand the relation the mind sustains to the body. If the system is deranged by improper food, the brain and nerves are affected, and slight things annoy those who are thus afflicted. Little difficulties are to them troubles mountain high. Persons thus situated are unfitted to properly train their children. Their life will be marked with extremes, sometimes very indulgent, at other times severe, censuring for trifles which deserved no notice."—*Selected Messages,* book 2, p. 434.

Mother, the next time that Jimmy brings home an unsatisfactory report card, withhold your censure until you have studied the eating habits of your family and made out a nutritional report card for yourself. It just might be that the kind of meals you served your son determined the kind of grades he received. It just might be that you are the one who deserves the poor marks.

[1]. *Color Country Spectrum,* Sept. 23, 1979, p. 12.
[2]. Fred L. Phlegar and Barbara Phlegar, "Diet and Schoolchildren," *Phi Delta Kappan,* September, 1979, p. 54.
[3]. *Ibid.,* p. 53.
[4]. *Ibid.,* p. 54.
[5]. Napa *Register,* March 25, 1977.
[6]. Bakersfield *Californian,* Oct. 7, 1979.
[7]. Phlegar and Phlegar, *op. cit.,* p. 54.

"To Santa Claus and Little Sisters"

*H*e was only 15 when he wrote the poem. Two years later he committed suicide.

"To Santa Claus and Little Sisters" was a strange poem. It was about three other poems he had written.

The first was about his dog, Chops. He showed it to his mother, and she hung it on the kitchen door and read it to his aunts.

The second poem was called "Question Marked Innocence." He didn't show this one to his mother, because he didn't want it hung on a door or shared with others.

He did show it to his teacher. After the man read it he gave the boy "a strange, steady look." Then he scrawled an A at the top of the page.

The third poem was about nothing. That's the way the boy described it. "Absolutely nothing." He had wanted to carry it to the kitchen, but couldn't. He had slashed his wrists in the bathroom.

Abraham Blinderman, professor of English at the State University of New York, studied the poem after the young poet had died and found that it indicated deep distress. It was a cry for help.[1]

The boy had found life to be nothing. That's what the poem was all about. But nobody had understood. Not his mother. Not his aunts. Not his teacher. Perhaps that's why he had addressed the poem to Santa Claus and little sisters. They wouldn't understand either.

"Life is nothing. Absolutely nothing." This is what thousands of young people decided last year and the year before that and the year before that. This is what a young man decided some eight years after he had been my pupil. He was a bright, personable, cooperative child. Little did I realize that he would become a troubled teen-ager and would decide that life was purposeless and meaningless. One night he drove his car into a field, closed the windows, connected a hose to the exhaust, and extinguished nothingness.

In recent years so many young people have committed suicide that self-destruction has become the number two killer of youth. It has escalated 300 percent since 1960 and has become an alarming and monumental problem.

The fact that many youth are finding life to be meaningless was affirmed by a study conducted by Prof. Ralph Larkin, a Rutgers University sociologist. Oxford University Press published his 259-page report, *Suburban Youth in Cultural Crisis.* It contains the results of interviews conducted in 1976 at a high school in an affluent suburb near New York City. To keep the true identity of the institution secret, Larkin named it Utopia High School. As a result of his interviews with students, he concluded: "The major problem that young people at Utopia High must face is . . . lack of meaning in their lives."

Larkin's report only puts into focus a fact of which we have become uncomfortably aware: Youth are plagued by the questions Who am I? Why am I here? What does it all mean? How do I get it all together?

In an article entitled "Why Students Turn to Drugs," published in a national magazine, a Yale University student wrote: "Drugs looked like an answer to many bewildering questions I faced. They would, I thought, tell me who I was and where my life was going."

As youth seek unsuccessfully for answers to these basic questions, they may turn to deviant behavior. It is symptomatic of the deeper problem: being unable to get it all together.

Indicative of deviancy is the fact that drug abuse is the most serious problem facing teen-agers. There has been such a marked increase in drinking that an estimated 19 percent of high school students have become problem drinkers.

There is now an epidemic of illegitimate births throughout the Nation. The ratio of extramarital births to all those among both blacks and whites has doubled since the mid-1960s. Our country now has more unmarried mothers than widowed mothers. Fifty-two percent of all black children and 16 percent of whites live in fatherless homes.

Why are so many youth having problems in the conduct of their personal lives? Why do so many feel adrift and without purpose and meaning? Why, at a time when young people normally would be anticipating fulfillment of life, are they increasingly committing suicide?

A formidable reason is the increasing devaluation of human life. In earlier decades Western culture stressed individual worth. Reference was made to "the sanctity of human life." The Judeo-Christian culture taught that man was made in the image of God and was a child of God. Consequently each human being had intrinsic worth, unique value, as a person. As a child of God man was spiritually rooted. He was "the son of Seth, which was the son of Adam, which was the son of God" (Luke 3:38). He had not only identity but also the corollaries of this identity: absolutes that gave him a framework of values, fixed guidelines as a basis for making choices.

Young people were taught Biblical standards of conduct. The established authorities, the so-called ancestral order—the home, the school, the church—were the powerful educators, particularly in the area of values. These institutions were coherent and reenforcing, affirming like values and teaching them to youth. Young people knew what was right and what was wrong. They knew where the fences were—and the barbed wire. Even though some might reject the fixed guidelines, there was "the light and the leading, the guidance and the support, the discipline that the ancestral order provided."

Youth: Is it all right for unmarried men and women to live together?

The Established Authority: No! God forbids extramarital sex. "Thou shalt not commit adultery" (Ex. 20:14).

Youth: Is homosexuality just a matter of sexual preference?

The Established Authority: No! Homosexuality is sin. The Bible denounces it as perversion. Concerning it Paul said: "In consequence, I say, God has given them up to shameful passions.

Their women have exchanged natural intercourse for unnatural, and their men in turn, giving up natural relations with women, burn with lust for one another; males behave indecently with males, and are paid in their own persons the fitting wage of such perversion" (Rom. 1:26, 27, N.E.B.).

Youth: If I want to read immoral publications or go to X-rated movies, it's my right, isn't it?

The Established Authority: No! You are not sovereign of yourself. "In him we live, and move, and have our being" (Acts 17:28). God has given us a standard by which to make our choices: "Finally, brethren, whatsoever things are true, whatsoever things are honest, whatsoever things are just, whatsoever things are pure, whatsoever things are lovely, whatsoever things are of good report; if there be any virtue, and if there be any praise, think on these things" (Phil. 4:8).

As the evolutionary hypothesis became increasingly accepted, man was uprooted spiritually. No longer was he the son of Adam, who was the son of God. Darwinism made of man an incidental product of the world process, a chance arrangement of neutrons and protons. As a biological accident, man had no purposeful beginning and, consequently, no purposeful ending. He was adrift.

Humanism replaced the traditional Judeo-Christian culture. With the dethronement of God came the uprooting of the traditional absolutes, the fixed guidelines for making choices. Secularism eroded the power of the ancestral order—the home, the school, the church. Erosion was not so much by supplanting these institutions, but rather by permeating them. Instead of withstanding secularism and its attendant permissiveness, the ancestral order embraced them. Among the casualties was the home.

"Suddenly I was sad." The home, once a refuge from the harshness of the outside world, became fragmented, a fragmentation that brought pain and damage to youth. Much of this resulted from an escalating divorce rate, which more than doubled in this country during a recent twelve-year period. It is a painful fact of life for 12 million youngsters in the United States. Children involved in the trauma of family breakup often experience a deep

sense of loss. They feel vulnerable to forces beyond their control. They are torn between conflicting loyalties, and at times they are neglected by troubled parents. Often they are removed from familiar surroundings.

An 8-year-old girl had this reaction to her parents' separation:

"I remember it was near my birthday when I was going to be 6 that Dad said at lunch he was leaving. I tried to say, 'No, Dad, don't do it,' but I couldn't get my voice out. . . . My life sort of changed at that moment. . . . I used to be always happy and suddenly I was sad." [2]

A 9-year-old girl said: "In a way, I thought I'd made it happen. I thought maybe I'd acted mean to my mother and my sister and I was being punished by God. So I tried to be really good by not waking Mom before schooltime and getting my own breakfast, and maybe God would change His mind. But it's been three years now, and I'm used to it all. Sometimes, when I make a wish with an eyelash, though, I still wish for Dad to come home." [3]

A 15-year-old expressed it this way: "You never feel permanent anymore. . . . You go from place to place. And I don't feel at home at Dad's. I feel very strange when his girlfriend is around." [4]

Another factor in the deterioration of the home is the widespread use of alcohol. Alcoholism is increasing among both men and women. Federal health officials estimate that one of every three Americans with a drinking problem is a woman, compared with one in six a decade ago. These are sobering statistics.

Parents who drink heavily are unable to perform the duties of parenthood. Their children live in uncertainty, fear, and humiliation. They are often neglected and the victims of abusive treatment. And whenever the child is subjected to long-term high-level stress, it is bound to affect his ability to perform in the classroom.

Other disruptive factors are weakening the home. When both parents work, children are left with sitters or are taken to day-care centers. Although the physical needs of the children may be met adequately, there are deeper individual needs that often are not satisfied.

It should also be noted that during this decade parental rejection of children has increased alarmingly. Rearing a child is commonly regarded as an unrelieved chore. Too many parents are thinking of their own needs rather than the needs of their children. Increasingly, personal gratification has become the value scale by which both men and women measure everything. Many of those who put personal gratification first are parents.

"Sensitive children see this behavior in their parents and turn away from their roots," wrote Robert Coles, one of the Nation's most eminent and influential child psychologists. "They drug themselves or knock themselves out with liquor or run away. They are running away from neglect and abuse by parents who are so wrapped up in their own personal trajectories that they don't offer their children some moral and spiritual vision to hold on to and to try to live up to. How many children are asked in a family setting such questions as: 'What is the meaning of life?' Instead, we're too busy trying to 'adjust' and figure out what we can get today and tomorrow." [5]

Just the facts. The school must share some of the blame for the fact that large numbers of young people are unequipped to deal with the problems of their personal lives, are unable to get it all together. Traditionally, the school was a powerful affirmer of values, a source of guidance, support, and discipline. Today's schools are highly secularized institutions. Few faculties concern themselves with giving their students a value system, a basis for knowing what is right and what is wrong. Too many educators themselves are secularists and abet, rather than counteract, permissiveness.

Referring to the schools' failure to expose students to values, Steven Muller, president of Johns Hopkins University in Baltimore, stated that universities are turning out highly skilled barbarians. No value framework is being provided for youth who are more and more searching for it. . . . People are looking for something that isn't there and find it difficult to function without it. [6]

An example of the schools' deliberate lack of moral teaching, a fear of telling students what is right and what is wrong, is found in the instruction given to teachers of sex education.

The manuals for teachers caution them not to use such words

as *right* and *wrong, good* and *bad,* when deviant sexual behavior is being discussed. They are told not to moralize, not to be judgmental, not to be personally committed, lest a guilt complex be instilled, lest it unfavorably affect self-image. They are told to present facts only, and to allow students to reach their own conclusions.

After the students have reached their own conclusions, based on the facts only, what then? Where is the measuring rod by which these youth are to test the validity of their deductions? There is none, and this is the most tragic aspect of sex education in the public schools. Each youth is left adrift with his own conclusions, each with his own ideas.

To tell adults just to present the facts—not to moralize or to be judgmental—is to demean the comprehension and judgment that they have for years been acquiring. There is no point in having maturity and greater insights if, instead of using these to help and guide youth, adults are asked to disregard them.

Youths' most tragic betrayal. There was a time when the church was the highest authority in giving man a framework of values, of fixed guidelines as a basis for making choices. These values were "the light and the leading." They were moral absolutes, a divine law that defined right and wrong for all men, for all times, for all places. But the church no longer teaches that these divine absolutes are inviolate. Increasingly, the church either outrightly rejects Scripture or accommodates it to the carnality of the human heart.

Many within the church no longer believe that the Bible is God's word in all that it teaches—or that it is the sole guide to standards of morality. Increasingly, through compromise and conciliation, the church has encouraged a spirit of opposition to Biblical teaching, of exaltation of human wisdom above the divine revelation. Consequently the line of demarcation between the church and the world has largely been obliterated. When worldlings unite with the church, they find they are among people just like themselves. They see only their own image. They hear only a playback of their own voices: a playback of conflicting and competing values and ideologies. This is a profound disillusionment. It is also the most tragic betrayal of youth.

Because our institutions have lost their coherent sense of values, youths feel a tremendous sense of alienation and insecurity. They yearn for answers to questions that plague them and cause anxiety. But the answers they receive are discordant and conflicting.

Youth: Is it all right for unmarried men and women to live together?

Conflicting Ideologies: Yes! No! It just depends on the situation . . . It is sin! The Bible condemns it . . . It is a way to become a more fully developed human being . . .

Youth: Is homosexuality just a matter of sexual preference?

Conflicting Ideologies: No! Yes! If you think it is all right, then for you it is all right. Each person has a right to decide for himself whether an action is right or wrong . . . It is perversion! God forbids it! . . . It's a matter of genes. People do what they do because of the makeup of their genes . . .

Youth: Is it wrong to read immoral publications and to attend X- or R-rated movies?

Conflicting Ideologies: No! Yes! If you wish to pollute yourself, it's your business . . . It's evil! "Blessed are the pure in heart: for they shall see God" (Matt. 5:8).

Betrayed by the home. Betrayed by the school. Betrayed by the church. Little wonder that youth are looking for something that isn't there. Little wonder that 40 percent of our teen-agers have turned to astrology for guidance. According to Gallup Organized Youth Survey Service, 10 million young people in the United States believe that heavenly bodies determine destinies. This pseudoscience flourished during the Dark Ages, a time of rampant superstition. It is a sad commentary on contemporary values that it should also flourish at a time of so-called intellectual enlighten-ment—and in the Nation that has as its motto "In God We Trust."

Little wonder that many youth have turned to the cults. These offer them the absolutes for which they yearn and search. And even though the price of uniting with the cultists is abject servitude, many young people are willing to pay the price in exchange for promised certainties.

Little wonder that an increasing number of youth write letters to Santa Claus and little sisters—and then extinguish nothingness.

" 'He wanted a destination, a pleasant termination. But he didn't know where, Or why, or how.' " [7]

So that parents who read this book may not have children who are unanchored and adrift—and who will not write letters to Santa Claus and little sisters—the following chapter discusses ways by which they can guide them to have life purpose and meaning.

---

[1] "To Santa Claus and Little Sisters," *Time,* March 13, 1972, p. 45.
[2] "The Children of Divorce," *Newsweek,* Feb. 11, 1980, p. 58.
[3] *Ibid.,* p. 59.
[4] *Ibid.,* p. 61.
[5] "Our Self-centered Children—Heirs of the 'Me' Decade," *U.S. News and World Report,* Feb. 25, 1980, p. 81.
[6] " 'Universities Are Turning Out Highly Skilled Barbarians,' " *U.S. News and World Report,* Nov. 10, 1980, p. 57.
[7] In John Stone, "He Wanted a Destination," *Insight,* Sept. 26, 1972.

Light a Candle

As was mentioned in a previous chapter, a class of teen-agers was asked to work together on developing advice they would like to give to their parents. One of the items on the list was a request that mother and father "light a candle. Show us the way. . . . If you don't believe in God, then tell us what you do believe in. We need to believe in something higher and stronger than ourselves."

To light a candle—to kindle faith—in the mind and heart of children is the most consequential challenge of parenthood. For both the earthly and eternal destiny of the child is determined by the way the candle is lighted.

How do parents light the candle? How do they go about building a spiritual foundation that will give their children's lives meaning and purpose, a faith that will be a stronghold against stress and sorrow, against evil and temptation?

As anthropologists point out, children are born "neutral." Their attitudes and ways of thinking are learned. Being a terrorist is a learned behavior. So is being a saint. Children are shaped as human beings largely by what their culture and human environment do to and for them. Particularly in the early years parents are largely the human environment. They are the shapers. As Donald F. Smith observed: "The way we are taught to think about the world we live in and about the people with whom we interact is the critical factor in our subsequent behavior. In short, we become what we are trained to become, not what we are born."

I attended a parent-teacher meeting at which the speaker was a college professor. Not only was he a popular teacher but he and his wife were prominent members of a nearby community. During his talk he said that he and his wife did not instruct their son, an only child, in any religious belief. "When he is older he can decide for himself what he wants to believe. We feel it is unfair to impose religious ideas and convictions on him when he is too young to think for himself."

One evening about ten years later, while reading the paper, I saw the picture of this man and his wife. They were on the steps of the county courthouse, about to enter the building to attend the trial of their son, who had been charged with trafficking in illegal drugs.

As I looked at those grim faces, I remembered the words the father had spoken at the meeting: "When he is older he can decide for himself what he wants to believe."

Would this boy have been tried and convicted for lawbreaking if his parents had given him guidance in the early years of life? If they had shared religious ideas and convictions with him? We cannot be sure, but we cannot help wondering, "How then shall they call on him in whom they have not believed? and how shall they believe in him of whom they have not heard?" (Rom. 10:14).

It is impossible for children to grow up without religious convictions of some kind. If their parents do not instruct them in truth there will be others to instruct them in error. Either the parents will sow seeds of righteousness or Satan will sow seeds of evil. It is one or the other.

> I must not interfere with any child,
> I have been told,
> To bend his will to mine or try
> To shape him in some mould
> Of thought.
> Naturally as a flower he must unfold.
> Yet flowers have the discipline
> Of wind and rain,
> And though I know it gives
> The gardener pain,
> I've seen him use his pruning shears
> To gain
> More strength and beauty for a blossom

bright.
And he would do whatever he
Thought right
To save his flowers from
A deadening blight.
I do not know, yet it does
Seem to me
That only weeds unfold
Just naturally.[1]

The time to light the candle is in infancy. Orientation to a value system and to life's meaning and purpose should begin even before the reasoning powers of the child have developed. Before a child can speak or understand speech, he is influenced by the spirit of the home. The words, the acts, and the behavior of the parents—even the expressions on their faces—influence the emotional attitudes of those within the home.

"What the child sees and hears is drawing deep lines upon the tender mind, which no after circumstances in life can entirely efface."—*Child Guidance,* p. 199.

The type of music that comes from the radio and stereo, the kind of sights and sounds that come from the television, help to create a home atmosphere. They are "drawing deep lines upon the tender mind." So are the pictures that hang on the walls.

Pictures can make a profound impression on the tender mind. When I was a child we sometimes visited relatives who had a picture in their living room that I shall never forget. It depicted a forest fire. In the forefront was a deer, panic-stricken by the flames and the heat. Behind the deer were frightened, howling wolves. This picture frightened me. Were I an artist, even now I could reproduce the details of it, so deep an impression did it make on my young mind.

Pictures can have either a good or a bad influence on the developing mind. A wise choice helps to instill values. In the McLin-Larson book *Creative Ideas for Child Training,* a caring mother was quoted as having said: "I believed that the pictures I hung in my children's rooms were important. In my son's bedroom I had a picture of Jesus in the Garden of Gethsemane. I put up no pictures of clowns or that kind of thing. In my daughter's bedroom was a picture of a nurse. She is now a registered nurse. I think pictures play a definite role in the thinking and growth of a child."[2]

In the same book, another mother wrote: "Everything we do for our children must be Christ-centered. The pictures in our children's rooms are pictures of Christ, pictures that help them to learn about Christ. Keeping Christ before them is our aim, and a wise choice of pictures helps in this."[3]

Why not hang a picture of Jesus with the children? Hang it where it will be the first thing your child sees when he awakens and the last thing he sees before going to sleep. Tell him the story of Jesus and the children. Explain to him that Jesus loves the children of today just as much as He loved the children of long ago. He wants children now to draw close to Him, too. He says, "Sue, come close to Me. John, I want you near." Tell them that the way we draw close to Him today is through prayer. This is the way we visit with Him now.

As Ellen White says in *Child Guidance:* "One of the first sounds that should attract . . . [the children's] attention is the name of Jesus, and in their earliest years they should be led to the footstool of prayer."—Page 488.

When you light the candle of faith in your child, be sure you light it with love and not with fear. All too often an adult's relationship to God is sustained by fear, because of faulty orientation in childhood. For many years this was true of Mary, a child of nonreligious parents.

Mary had an aunt and uncle who were devout, zealous Christians, and sometimes her parents left her with them. At such times these people felt they should make up for the fact that Mary received no religious instruction at home. They were well-meaning persons, but they had little understanding of how to light the candle of faith in a child. Their way of teaching Mary oriented her to fear God rather than to love Him. During one visit, Aunt Nell told Mary about the seven last plagues and the fate of the wicked. Another time she told her about the beasts of Daniel 7. She had a book that contained drawings of the beasts, and she showed these to Mary. The child was too young to understand her aunt's explanation of what the beasts symbolized. All that Mary was aware of was that they were dreadful and had something to do with God. They frightened her, and she cried.

The unfortunate orientation that Mary received remained with her for years. She told friends that the most formidable challenge of her Christian experience was to learn to love God rather than to fear Him.

There are many children who have had the character of God misrepresented to them. When 9-year-old Jeff was asked why he had been baptized he replied, "So I won't go to hell." His baptism was fear-compelled rather than love-impelled. Children who have had a fear of God instilled in them can be inclined toward emotional illness in later life, for fear is a poison that creates a state of mind in which there is anxiety, unease, dread. As is true of all negative emotions, fear not only haunts the mind but also adversely affects the body. True faith dispels negative emotions. It brings peace, trust, assurance. "There is no fear in love; but perfect love casteth out fear" (1 John 4:18).

Parents also misrepresent God to their children when they deal harshly and unkindly with them. This is because parents stand in the place of God, representing His character to them. How can children who have severe, censorious parents understand that God is tenderhearted? What does *tenderhearted* mean? How can children who are verbally and physically abused understand that God is love? What is love? These unfortunate children can understand much better such concepts as God of anger, God of vengeance. These are character attributes with which they are familiar.

"The minds of the little ones may be taught to turn to Jesus as the flower turns its opening petals to the sun."—*Ibid.,* p. 487. However, if the minds of the little ones are to turn to God "as the flower turns its opening petals to the sun," the true character of God must be presented to them.

From infancy every lesson taught to the child should be love-centered and Christ-centered. Jesus should be presented to them as the Good Shepherd, the Friend of children. Such teaching in no way minimizes the importance of teaching children to obey God. Rather, it gives them the impelling motive for obedience— love rather than fear.

From the earliest years children should be taught that God is loving and caring, ever ready to help and support His children. A family traveling in Alaska had an experience that indicated how well the parents had influenced their children to have complete trust and confidence in God.

It was night, and they were on an isolated road when their jeep became stuck in a snowbank. No help was available. It was -30° F., and the car heater wouldn't work. The father and son worked four hours on the jeep, but had no success. All of them were in pain from the numbing cold. The son came and opened the car door. Hardly able to speak, he said, "Keep praying, Mom."

The daughter said, "He knows we're here. It must be that we are being tested. But even if we don't get out—even if we should die—we know we can trust ourselves to Him."

Suddenly Mom remembered something she had read once in the book *Wilderness Parish*. The author had been in a similar situation and had done something that had worked. She called out the instruction to her husband. He did as she suggested, and soon the jeep was freed from the snowbank and they were on their way.

These children had been oriented to a meaningful faith. Confidence in God had been instilled in them, a confidence that could brave and accept death. Their parents had lighted well the candle of faith.

---

[1] Alice Judd, *Phi Delta Kappan*, January, 1981, p. 356. © January, 1981, Phi Delta Kappan, Inc.
[2] Page 26.
[3] *Ibid.*

More Candles to Light

My husband and I were once guests in a home that had evening devotions. There were two young children in the home, about 6 and 8 years old. When it was time for worship we gathered in the living room. First, Father read several long passages from the Bible. There was no discussion of what he had read. He also picked the song, chosen from the adult hymnal. He then led out in a long prayer, followed by Mother. Then Father boomed, "Teddy!" Teddy wavered a prayer. There was another boom, "Jim!" Jim dutifully obliged. Other than the commanded prayers, the children were given no opportunity to participate. They sat circumspectly on their chairs, obediently listening as they were expected to. To them the service must have seemed "as dry as the hills of Gilboa."

It was a service that must have pleased Satan. An accumulation of such services would result in young people who associate the character of God with everything that is stern and cheerless.

How different was the worship period in the Hoppe home and with what a different spirit! Rhonda Hoppe was a student at Pacific Union College in California when she wrote an aritcle in the *Adventist Review* about the happy family worship services that were held in her childhood home.

"It was worshiptime in the Hoppe household," she wrote. "The family were gathered in the living room. Brenda was snuggled on mother's lap, and I sat between mother and dad. The joyful strains of our childish voices blended with the voices of our parents as we sang: 'With Jesus in the family, Happy, happy home, Happy, happy home, Happy, happy home. . . .'

"Then we listened as daddy read us our Sabbath school lesson. Together we learned the memory verse for the week. Then it was time to talk to Jesus. We knelt in a circle and joined hands as we presented our praise and requests to our heavenly Father." [1]

Counsel given in the book *Child Guidance* states: "The father, who is the priest of his household, should conduct the morning and evening worship. There is no reason why this should not be the most interesting and enjoyable exercise of the home life, and God is dishonored when it is made dry and irksome. Let the seasons of family worship be short and spirited. Do not let your children or any member of your family dread them because of their tediousness or lack of interest. When a long chapter is read and explained and a long prayer offered, this precious service becomes wearisome, and it is a relief when it is over."—Page 521.

The spirit in which family worship is conducted will help to determine its impact on the children. It should be happy and cheerful. The children should be aware of kindliness and affection. The service should be a time when family members draw close to one another and close to God. It is not a time for scolding and condemnation.

Suppose that during your devotional periods the children tend to be restless and inattentive. Suppose that one evening Father is piqued because the youngsters are not listening. He snaps angrily, "You are not paying attention. Go to your rooms and stay there!"

The children go to their rooms and stay there. What will this unfortunate episode do to their attitude toward family worship? Will it encourage an interest in devotions? Or will it kindle antagonism?

Inattention and restlessness are indications that something is wrong with the worship service. Instead of reprimanding the children, parents should ask themselves some questions. Why are the children inattentive? Why are they fidgety? What can we do to make our devotions more meaningful and interesting?

So that family worship will be pleasant and profitable, a time of family warmth and spiritual strengthening, parents might like to consider the following suggestions:

Adapt the worship service to the maturity level of the children. Is what you present suitable for the occasion? Family worship is hardly the place to interpret the beasts of Daniel 7 or to unravel the mystery of the 144,000 of Revelation 14.

Use visual aids to make your teaching more graphic: pictures, objects, a felt board, a blackboard. These are attention-getters and will vitalize your teaching.

Vary your worship service. By changing the regular order of things, devotions won't be a mere form, a dull, monotonous repetition.

Avoid long-drawn-out devotions. Tediousness results when the service is too long. It wearies the mind of the children. Short, meaningful devotions hold interest and create more lasting impressions.

Have the children participate in the service. Family worship shouldn't be a solo performance. Active participation on the part of the children is the best remedy for boredom. Let them have a part in prayer and take turns choosing a song. If it's the month of July and Kate wants to sing "O Little Town of Bethlehem," don't say, "Kate, we don't sing Christmas songs in July." That doesn't matter. What is important is that it is *her* selection. It's a song *she* likes. If she is aware that you like it too, she will be happy. Family devotions will be associated with happy feelings.

At times let the children present the devotional. They can read or tell a favorite Bible story or perhaps read a short story from their church paper. When they are older, give them a turn in planning and leading out in the service.

Don't forget that your toddler wants to do something. He can have the privilege of getting the Bible from its place and taking it to Daddy. This will make the service more meaningful to him.

Make Bible instruction relevant. Unless children can see that the lessons of the Bible apply to their own lives—can be incorporated into their own experiences—the Bible will not be to them living words. Nor will the God of heaven be a living God in whom they "live, and move, and have . . . [their] being." Only when God and the things of God become living realities, relevant to the here and now, will faith be "an anchor that keeps the soul." Only then will it endure when it is assailed by life's reverses. For this reason it is of the utmost importance that parents vitalize their Bible teaching so that it isn't merely lifeless tales about long-ago people.

Teach children heavenly truth through things with which they are familiar. Use the *known* to teach the *unknown*. This was the principle of teaching that Jesus used. He linked divine truth with the ordinary things and incidents that were familiar to the people. "Consider the lilies of the field." "Behold, a sower went forth to sow." "There was a certain householder, which planted a vineyard."

Suppose that the memory verse to be learned during worship is 1 Samuel 2:30: "Them that honour me I will honour." Through discussion and questioning, guide the children to see the relevancy of this text to their own experience. "Johnny, if your teacher gives a test tomorrow and the boy who sits next to you wants to cheat, what could you do that would honor God so that He could honor you?"

"Lisa, if Susie starts to tell you unkind things about Sharon, what could you do that would honor God so that He could honor you?"

Encourage independent thinking. Guide your children to perceive truth for themselves. Minds that rely upon other minds will sooner or later be misguided. When Jesus created the flowers, why didn't He make them all the same color? Why do you think that Lot's wife looked back? Why do you think Moses struck the rock instead of speaking to it as God had directed? Questions like these challenge the thinking of your children.

Worship services are a fine time to teach children texts of comfort and promise. "God is our refuge and strength, a very present help in trouble" (Ps. 46:1). "I will turn their mourning into joy, and will comfort them" (Jer. 31:13).

A missionary wife once took the mission children on an outing. A pack of barking dogs came up to them. It was a time of stress and danger—but not for a little girl named Jennie. She came to the missionary and said, " 'What time I am afraid, I will trust in thee.' " The missionary had taught Jennie this verse.[2] She had taught her so well that the child, in a time of danger, turned "to Jesus as the flower turns its opening petals to the sun."

It is important to make the texts meaningful to the children at their present level of development. All too often Bible verses are taught with the idea that they will be sustaining in later life. If they are taught with relevancy they can be just as sustaining at the children's present level. For this reason, "teach the young tendrils to twine about God for support."—*Child Guidance,* p. 31.

Children have many disappointments. When Mary wasn't invited to Cora's birthday party, it hurt her just as much as it hurt Mother when she wasn't invited to Mrs. Johnson's luncheon. When Sammy didn't make the team, it hurt him just as much as it hurt Daddy when he didn't get the promotion he had anticipated. At such times, remembering texts of promise and comfort will be "a very present help in trouble."

To make Scripture relevant and meaningful, at times insert the children's names in the texts. After a verse has been learned, personalize it. " 'Be thou faithful unto death,' Lois, 'and I will give thee a crown of life.' " " 'If ye love me,' Kathy, 'keep my commandments.' " " 'If we confess our sins,' Timmy, 'he is faithful and just to forgive us our sins.' " Personalizing the texts makes God seem near. It helps to dispel the thought that He is a faraway God, too far removed to be concerned about the people of earth.

It is well to mention each child by name in your prayer at worship. "Thank You, God, for giving us Nell and Ronnie. Our home would be a very lonesome place without them. We love them very much. Please help us to be good parents to them."

Will children ever forget prayers such as this? Won't such prayers help to bind them to their parents? In later life, might not the memory of such prayers make the difference between faithfulness and apostasy?

Vitalizing your family worship will help to strengthen your children spiritually. It will help to build in them a sure foundation, an anchor for their souls. It will help to light candles of faith that will burn brightly throughout their lives.

---

[1] Rhonda Hoppe, "When God Comes Looking," *Adventist Review,* Feb. 15, 1979.
[2] Ruth McLin and Jeanne Larson, *Creative Ideas for Child Training,* p. 24.

To Johnny, With Love

*T*here are gifts for children more important and meaningful than any that can be wrapped in paper and tied with ribbon. Long after other gifts have been outgrown or outworn, these will endure. They will last as long as the child to whom they were presented lives. These gifts should be the birthright of every son and daughter, but too many of today's parents are forgetting them. Why not check your list to make certain that you have remembered to include gifts such as these:

To Mary, from Mother and Father: *more of our time.* Our determination to see that our home is more than merely a house in which to stay long enough to change our clothes. Our realization that satisfying only physical needs is not enough. We must make provision for the heart's hunger.

To Tony, from Mother and Father: *our example.* Patterns of life in which you will see the exemplification of all the moral and ethical concepts that we have upheld before you.

To Jenny, from Mother and Father: *goals toward purposeful living.* Goals that put more emphasis on individual worth and on service to fellow men than on competitive striving, the acquisition of possessions, and thoughtless conformity to artificial standards.

To Sally, from Mother and Father: *acceptance of life as a challenge and a trust.* Help to discover meaning in the everyday tasks of life and to find satisfaction in simple, natural things.

To Linda, from Mother and Father: *a faith to live by.* A faith that will be a bulwark against the disenchantment of later years. A rock of ages for shelter in times of stress.

To Andy, from Mother and Father: *our acceptance of you just as you are.* Our help toward the realization of all your potentials, but our promise that we will not compare you unfavorably with children who may have been endowed with more talents. We will not accept less than your best, but we will not censure you because your best does not coincide with our self-esteem and ego.

To David, from Mother and Father: *all of our love.* The realization that we want, enjoy, and love you. The sure knowledge that you mean a great deal to us and that we are concerned about what happens to you.

Your children will receive many gifts during the years that they are with you. Will they also receive these more enduring gifts of the Spirit?